Vlad the Impaler

A Captivating Guide to How Vlad III Dracula Became One of the Most Crucial Rulers of Wallachia and His Impact on the History of Romania

Free Bonus from Captivating History (Available for a Limited time)

Hi History Lovers!

Now you have a chance to join our exclusive history list so you can get your first history ebook for free as well as discounts and a potential to get more history books for free! Simply visit the link below to join.

Captivatinghistory.com/ebook

Also, make sure to follow us on Facebook, Twitter and Youtube by searching for Captivating History.

Contents

Introduction

The medieval Balkans almost seem like uncharted territory to Western historians. Modern events such as the collapse of the Eastern Bloc, the Yugoslav Wars, the tension with the migrant crisis, and the hostilities between nations overshadow the fact that this area, which connects Asia Minor to Central Europe, is rich with a turbulent, bloody, and fascinating history. Some of the biggest and most important battles were fought in the medieval Balkans, resulting in a series of notable demographic and political changes that resonated throughout the rest of the continent.

But the Balkans aren't mysterious simply due to its history. Another phenomenon seemed to have taken Europe by storm that originated from this area, that of vampirism. Ever since the first official cases of vampiric activity among the Serbian populace were written about by Austro-Hungarian newspapers in the 18th century, Europe could not get enough of the blood-sucking fiends. Other stories resurfaced, but the vampire hysteria reached its peak with the publishing of one novel in 1897, a novel that spoke of supernatural beings in Victorian England but whose main antagonist bore the name, or rather the nickname, of a historical figure who had, at that point, been dead for over 400 years.

The Balkans were the home of both the vampiric stories and the aforementioned monarch, whose name became synonymous with drinking blood and avoiding sunlight. That monarch was Vlad, the third ruler of Wallachia to hold that name, the second ruler to be associated with the Order of the Dragon (and to incorporate that into his name), and the first ruler to be associated with a gruesome act, that of impalement. Vlad III, *Vlad Țepeș* in Romanian, also known as Vlad the Impaler or Vlad Dracula, was (and still is) a never-ending conversational piece among Romanian historians, medievalists, political analysts, literary critics, and even the common folk. This voivode ("prince" or "duke") from a small Balkan land would not only become a terrifying figure that some of even the most powerful monarchs at the time would fear but would also become a fascinating individual worthy of entire poems, legends, and art pieces being devoted to him. And despite ruling very briefly compared to other monarchs at the time, he still left a very notable imprint on the political and social life of his native medieval Wallachia, as well as the countries surrounding it. He would become a man to take the throne no less than three times, get captured and held as a prisoner for decades no less than twice during his life, a father to children whose descendants would rule Wallachia well over 200 years after his death, and a man whose heroic and patriotic acts were overshadowed by literally hundreds of thousands of corpses.

In this book, we will focus on the turbulent and fascinating life of Vlad the Impaler. Before we delve into it, however, a fair warning to the fans of Bram Stoker's novel should be issued. Though he wasn't a vampire himself, Vlad III did lead a life that would rival some of the best fictional characters out there. By reading onward, you might leave with the impression that Dracula, the figure who seduced young British women and bore himself as an aristocrat of elegance with a penchant to drink blood, pales in comparison to the historical figure he is merely based off of. That's right; this book will illustrate that Vlad the Impaler, a seemingly insignificant lord of a small nation who barely had a few years to his reign, has more appeal than a fictional monster with otherworldly powers.

Naturally, there are many details about Vlad's life that we simply do not know. Contemporary documents definitely exist, even some written by the man himself, but in terms of the necessary documentation to complete the picture, they are few and far between. In addition, there are decades of his life where almost nothing was written about him, making it even more difficult to maintain a single, unified image of Vlad. Fortunately, the interest for the voivode has not waned in the 21st century, as the scientific community keeps discovering new details about his life and adding to the significant wealth of information we already have.

The bulk of the book will deal with what Vlad's political career looked like, what wars he waged, and how his life eventually ended. But we'll go one step beyond and cover some areas that historians don't typically focus on. In addition to raw facts, we'll also focus on what Vlad III's character was, what drove him forward, and what his chief traits might have been. In addition, we will give a much-needed focus on his successors and what life was like in Wallachia after his passing. Furthermore, you'll also get a glimpse into some of the most popular myths and legends about Vlad III, some of which were written and passed on by both his supporters and his bitter enemies. All of these are needed to get as complete an image of Vlad as possible, which will help us understand what kind of man he was and what kind of impact his life had on those around him, as well as those who came after him.

Portrait of Vlad the Impaler at Ambras Castle, Innsbruck, Austria, circa 1560.

Chapter 1 – Early Years: Birth, Captivity, First Reign, and Exile; Wallachia and the Balkans in the Early 15th Century

Birth of Vlad III

The exact year of Vlad's birth is still debated among historians. In fact, most of the facts regarding the Impaler's life have to be pieced together from fragments of available information, considering that most of the official records kept in the Balkan countries from that time period have disappeared after the Ottoman invasions. At best, we can ascertain that he was born anywhere between 1429/1430 and 1436.

Interestingly enough, though we might not know the exact date of Vlad's birth, we have a reasonable idea of where he might have been born. Modern-day Sighişoara in Romania's province of Transylvania still contains a house that Vlad II Dracul, i.e., the father of Vlad the Impaler, supposedly lived in with his first-born son, Mircea.

The house and the town itself aren't arbitrarily chosen as the birthplace of Vlad the Impaler, of course. Sighișoara, then known as both Schaäsburg (in German) and Segesvár (in Hungarian), was an important trading and crafting hub of Transylvania. Over fifteen guilds and twenty handicraft branches found their home in the city, and Vlad Dracul himself minted coins there. The town was populated by both Wallachians and Hungarians, but a growing population of German artisans, originally from the Holy Roman Empire, made their home here as well. In fact, a significant part of Vlad's early childhood was spent in Transylvania among the local Saxon communities.

While most people today associate the Impaler with Transylvania, the truth is that Vlad was a Wallachian voivode, and most of his time spent in Transylvania did not see him rule over that land. During the early 15th century, Dracula and his family were predominantly Wallachian voivodes, but they did get involved in the state affairs of both Transylvania and neighboring Moldavia.

In order to understand the whole situation, we need to examine how the ancestors of modern Romanians and Moldovans went about their days during the Late Middle Ages. Both Wallachia and Moldavia were semi-independent lands that were predominantly inhabited by Romanian-speaking people who practiced Eastern Orthodox Christianity and were under the direct cultural influence of the Greeks (the Eastern Roman Empire, i.e., the Byzantines) and various Slavic groups (predominantly Bulgarians and Serbs). For example, most of their religious customs came from the Byzantines, but their court titles and architectural layouts of castles were mostly Slavic-like. In addition, Old Church Slavonic was the "diplomatic" language of the elites, and most rulers in this era wrote and spoke it (similar to semi-independent Albanian territories during the same timespan). However, the territory known as "the land beyond the forest" (*ultra sylvam*) isn't that easy to pinpoint in terms of populace. While it was definitely home to a large Wallachian population, from the early 11th century up until the modern day, the Wallachians were never a majority there. In fact, based on all the archeological evidence

and contemporary written sources, we can safely say that the majority of Transylvanians were not Wallachian, didn't speak or write predominantly in Slavic, and were the polar opposites of Eastern Orthodox Christians. Transylvania was officially a Hungarian vassal territory subjected to the Hungarian king, who had the power to instate his own voivodes as protectors of the land. However, the territory boasted a large number of German Saxon inhabitants who began to show up en masse during the beginning of the new millennium (Saxons also inhabited neighboring Serbia and Bulgaria, working largely as miners and smiths). Finally, there were the Székelys (referred to as Szeklers in further text), a sub-group of Hungarians whose origins are still somewhat debated but who served as frontier guards for the Kingdom of Hungary during the Early Middle Ages. All three groups were primarily Catholic and swore loyalty to the Hungarian Crown, often acting in direct opposition to any Wallachian voivode who would come to power.

The reason the composition of the populace of Transylvania is important for the history of Vlad the Impaler is due to the fact that it shaped most of his later worldviews. We'll delve more into this in later chapters, but to sum it up, Vlad was someone who grew up in a multiethnic environment with diametrically opposing religious and cultural beliefs, and while he did work hard on ensuring the stability and well-being of his own multiethnic state, he was still as xenophobic and mistrusting as a medieval prince would be. And he's by no means alone in this: most medieval rulers throughout the world, on all permanently inhabited continents, were outright antagonistic toward neighboring tribes and would frequently exert efforts into assimilating or annihilating them.

Dracula's house in Sighişoară

Balkans in the Late 15th Century

As stated earlier, Vlad was most likely born between 1429 and 1436. It was a time of great turmoil within the Balkan Peninsula. The emerging Ottoman Empire kept growing in size and strength, and the effects of this growth were felt across the independent lands whose own influence was waning. The once-powerful Eastern Roman Empire had, by the 1450s, been reduced to a few territories in modern-day Greece and the territory of Constantinople, which had, by that point, become a shadow of its former self. The majority of its inhabitants were long gone, and from a perspective of a local citizen, it looked not unlike a ghost town. The incumbent emperors at the time, the Palaiologoi dynasty (sing. *Palaiologos*, meaning "old word"), were effectively vassals to the Turks. Not only would they have to pay a monetary tribute to the sultan, but they would also be subjugated to the system known as Devshirme, i.e., paying tribute "in blood." The system was simple enough: Ottoman troops would take a group of boys and young men between the ages of eight and twenty, transport them to a major Ottoman center, and forcefully convert them to Islam. Once they were Islamized, the boys would either become soldiers (as a part of the elite troops called the Janissaries) or would enter the civil service as diplomats and viziers. Hundreds of thousands of Christian boys were converted through this system until it was abolished in the early 18th century, with the vast majority of them being of Greek origin.

However, the Turks had other nations to deal with during the early years of Vlad's life. Right around the time of the collapse of the Eastern Roman Empire, Serbia had risen to prominence, having been elevated to the status of empire in 1346. After the fall of the empire several decades later and the famous Battle of Kosovo in 1389, Serbia became a vassal state of the Ottomans, with its territory greatly reduced and ruled by a despot (a royal title one rank below that of an emperor). Between 1427 and 1456, the despot would be Đurađ Branković, the first ruler of the Branković family to sit on the throne and the last effective ruler of the Serbian lands. At the age of fifty, he had the experience and the prowess of a decent ruler, as well as an incredible amount of wealth. However, his territory was independent in name only; just like the Palaiologoi, the Branković dynasty also had to pay tribute to the Ottomans. Still, he wasn't necessarily a loyal vassal of the empire, nor was he really loyal to their enemies. Though he maintained good relations with Sultan Murad II, largely because his daughter, Mara Branković, was married to the sultan in 1434, he was also a close ally to the Hungarian Crown, as well as the Republic of Venice and some parts of medieval Zeta. Of course, Đurađ Branković's rivalry with the Hungarian general and Christian hero John Hunyadi would result in him constantly either refusing to help the Christian cause against the Ottomans or even helping the Ottomans (such as when he captured Hunyadi after the lesser-known Second Battle of Kosovo in 1448 and kept his older son as a hostage for a ransom), which was, in and of itself, bizarre considering the exchange of estates between Hunyadi and Branković not too long ago. Both men would die in 1456, several months apart from one another. The death of Đurađ Branković was possibly the biggest blow to late medieval Serbia since a succession crisis ensued, with his remaining family members feuding over the inheritance. A mere three years later, the Serbian Despotate would finally succumb to the Turks, and the country would not regain its independence until the late 19th century.

Bosnia was in a similar situation to Serbia, with its reigning Kotromanić dynasty being weakened by regional rulers who tore the country apart. Its last ruler was Stephen II Tomašević, who was, interestingly enough, the last official despot of an independent Serbia before surrendering it to the Ottomans in 1459 and returning to his native Bosnia, where he was crowned as king soon after in 1461. His own death in 1463 at the hands of Sultan Mehmed II himself (or one of his close military officials), as well as the deaths of his closest living male family members, marked the end of Bosnia and the subsequent Ottoman rule that would last until the territories were annexed by Austria-Hungary in the late 19th and early 20th centuries.

Of all the Balkan-based lands, Hungary was probably the biggest rival of the Turks during Vlad's time. It was the Hungarian king, Sigismund of Luxembourg, who decided to act against the Ottomans by forming the so-called Order of the Dragon. This Order contained prominent members of European nobility, including Đurađ Branković's predecessor, Despot Stefan Lazarević (the son of Lazar Hrebeljanović, the Serbian prince who led the Serbian army against the Ottomans during the Battle of Kosovo in 1389); Hermann II, Count of Celje and the father-in-law of King Sigismund; Pippo Spano, an Italian general and magnate who was Sigismund's personal friend and a talented statesman; Karlo Kurjaković, a Croatian nobleman and one of the Order's founders; Fruzhin, a Bulgarian noble who was descended from the last Bulgarian emperors and who was a staunch fighter against the Turks; King Alfonso V of Aragon, an exceptionally important figure during the early Renaissance; Gjergj Kastrioti Skanderbeg, an Albanian noble who became renowned all over Europe for his fierce battles against the Ottoman troops; and Vlad II Dracul, Vlad the Impaler's father. In fact, Vlad's sobriquet "Dracul" actually derives from his position as a member of the Order, as it means "dragon." Subsequently, Vlad III's own sobriquet can be read as "little dragon" or "the son of the dragon."

Hungary's importance during the early years of Dracula's life cannot be overstated. Sigismund's general John Hunyadi, for example, had been so influential in the region that he was able to instate his own voivode in Transylvania, and after dethroning Vlad Dracul in 1447, he even referred to the contemporary Wallachian capital of Târgovişte as his city. Hunyadi's influence had been strong even within Hungary itself. As a regent of young Ladislaus V the Posthumous, the underage son of the late Albert II of Germany, who had been the legitimate heir of the late Sigismund of Luxembourg, Hunyadi had enjoyed a life of absolute privilege and was one of the richest men in the region at the time, wealthier than even some contemporary rulers. The people had admired Hunyadi so much that, not long after his death, his son Matthias Corvinus was declared king, following a bloody rebellion that caused the young king Ladislaus to flee Hungary, unexpectedly dying soon after. Corvinus himself would be instrumental in Vlad the Impaler's adult life, both as an enemy and as an ally.

Naturally, this is but a brief overview of some of the major players among the Balkan states in the Late Middle Ages, and it merely scratches the surface of the political picture at the time. Other countries, such as Bulgaria, Albania, Zeta, the Republic of Ragusa (today's city of Dubrovnik in Croatia), the Republic of Venice, and the semi-independent Croatian and Slovenian territories also played a vital role throughout the century, but covering everything would require a whole other book to be written. But based on these simplified examples above, we can clearly see just how convoluted the Balkan political scene was during these turbulent times. If we were to include the religious relations between the countries, their economic statuses, their day-to-day lives, major battles, forming of alliances and their break-ups, and so on, there would be no end to this book. And we should also take into account that most of the contemporary sources we have are often incomplete, contradictory, or outright fabricated. Naturally, Wallachia itself was just as complicated, which made Vlad's ascension(s) to the throne quite exciting but equally convoluted and dangerous.

Vlad's Childhood and Captivity under the Ottomans

As a child, Vlad was most likely taught the same things that his brothers Mircea and Radu were. At an early age, he had to be a skilled horse rider, sword fighter, and marksman; the knowledge of several languages was a must, especially in a region as diverse as the Balkan Peninsula, as well as the knowledge of several different scripts like Latin and Cyrillic. Moreover, there was the question of faith. With the Muslim Ottomans slowly encroaching on the Balkan states, it was of vital importance that Christianity prevailed. However, Wallachia was an Orthodox country, while Hungary, which was the overlord of Wallachia, was Catholic. Vlad's older brother Mircea was more than likely baptized in a Catholic church, but history isn't entirely sure about Vlad and Radu. Most likely, they were baptized secretly in an Orthodox church in Wallachia, but Vlad himself would convert to Catholicism some years before his death, which he did in order to prove his loyalty to the Hungarian Crown and to regain (and retain) his title of the Wallachian voivodeship.

By the age of eleven, young Vlad would have been taught several skills, including jousting, fencing, swimming, court etiquette, archery, and horse riding. By all accounts, he was a gifted and quick learner, acquiring all the necessary skills that a Balkan monarch needed at an early age. However, Vlad's early adolescence would prove to be a difficult one, mainly due to the dealings of his father. During the reign of Sigismund, Vlad II had been an ally of the Hungarians, becoming acquainted with some of the most prominent figures in Hungarian nobility, including John Hunyadi in his early years. Even in those days, Hunyadi was a cunning strategist and a favorite among the

16

Christian communities despite being a man born in low nobility and hailing from Wallachia (though there are conflicting sources over his origins, most scholars consider the Hunyadi family as ethnically Wallachian/Romanian). By the time Vlad II had ascended the throne, Hunyadi had already been in the service of the late Serbian despot Stefan Lazarević and had since been serving as one of Sigismund's most efficient military leaders. One of the many reasons why Hunyadi was so effective was his undying loyalty to the Christian faith and his desire to defend Christianity at all costs, a trait that would eventually put him at odds with Vlad II and start a chain of events that would affect young Vlad III.

As a ruler, Vlad II had been an enemy of the Ottomans during Sigismund's reign, but after the Hungarian king's death in 1437, he signed an alliance with the Turkish sultan Murad II, agreeing to pay him a yearly tribute of 10,000 ducats and provide military aid. This act on Vlad II's behalf was in direct contradiction with his obligations to the Order of the Dragon, whose name he still used. At the time, the united Christian effort wanted to engage in another crusade against the Ottomans, but Sigismund's death had led to a succession crisis. Several rulers were claimants and held the throne for a short time, including Albert II of Germany, who ruled roughly two years before dying of dysentery while preparing for a crusade; the infant Ladislaus the Posthumous, with his mother Elisabeth of Luxembourg (the only surviving child of King Sigismund) serving as a regent; and the Polish king Władysław III, a member of the Jagiellonian dynasty. Władysław was crowned in 1440 and was backed by Hunyadi, but Ladislaus was named as his successor should he die without issue. A year later, having somewhat secured the Hungarian throne and calmed the succession crisis a bit, Hunyadi visited Vlad II in Târgoviște in 1441. And even though he was sternly reminded that his loyalties should lie with the Order of the Dragon and the Christian cause, Vlad II still refused to end his relations with the Turks. However, oddly enough, he had only been a half-hearted ally of the sultan to begin with. When the Turks marched into Wallachia on their way to invade

Transylvania, Vlad II remained neutral, simply allowing them to pass. This action resulted in a humiliating defeat of the Turks and put further doubt into Murad II's mind when it came to the Wallachian voivode's loyalty. It didn't help matters that other local princes wrote to the sultan warning him not to trust Vlad, among other rulers.

Sometime between 1442 and 1443, Murad II decided to act on his suspicions and invited both Vlad II and Đurađ Branković to his court. The Serbian despot shrewdly avoided going, but the Wallachian voivode set out to see the sultan in the city of Gallipoli, taking his two youngest sons with him and leaving his oldest heir, Mircea, to rule during his absence. To young Vlad and the even younger Radu, this trip would prove to be one of the most traumatic events of their lives. Upon their arrival in Gallipoli, the voivode and his sons were put in chains. Vlad II himself was kept in the city dungeon, but his sons were sent to Eğrigöz (modern-day Doğrugöz in Turkey), a grim mountain fortress. All three would eventually end up in Adrianople, the Ottoman capital (modern-day Edirne), at the court of the sultan. Less than a year after his capture, Vlad II was made to swear an oath of loyalty to the Turkish court all over again, on both the Bible and the Quran, but this time, the tribute was more than a "mere" 10,000 ducats. In addition to the money, Vlad II had to send at least 500 young men under the Devshirme system, and more importantly, both young Vlad and Radu were to be kept as hostages at the sultan's court. That way, the Ottoman ruler had the means of directly punishing Vlad II should he not honor his tribute.

Of course, the deal that Murad II forced onto Vlad II offered some obligations on the sultan's part as well. As long as the Wallachian voivode did what he was told, no harm was to come to the boys. In addition, they were to receive the best education and the best treatment, just like any other child of an obedient nobleman. The young Dracul boys were taught everything from theoretical mathematics to basic precepts of the Quran and Aristotelian logic, as well as some of the fine Eastern Roman traditions that the Turks themselves inherited. Young Vlad's knowledge of the Turkish language also improved, which would prove invaluable in his future exploits. However, the two boys took to their captivity very differently. Even at this early age, Vlad was showing signs of disobedience to his Turkish overlords, often lashing out against his teachers and receiving severe punishments for it. Radu, however, became somewhat of a court favorite. Because of his outstanding good looks, he was to gain his own sobriquet of *Radu cel Frumos,* "Radu the Handsome," and would become a source of infatuation for both the women and men at the sultan's court. Some contemporary sources even mention that Murad's son, Mehmed II, treated Radu as his lover. Whatever the case might be, Radu proved to be more loyal to the Turks than either his father or his brothers, which would again prove to be instrumental in later years when Vlad III ascended to (and descended from) the throne multiple times.

During the captivity of the three Draculs, typical medieval Balkan politics once again shook the throne of Wallachia. The country itself was, at one point, ruled by the unified House of Basarab, named after the first independent ruler of Wallachia, Voivode Basarab I. However, after the death of Dan I, the step-uncle of Vlad II Dracul, the throne was succeeded by his step-brother Mircea, known in Wallachian history as Mircea the Old due to his long reign and the respect he commanded. Both Dan's and Mircea's descendants would constantly try to usurp the throne from one another, forming two main branches of the House of Basarab, called the House of Dăneşti and the House of Drăculeşti. And much like Vlad the Impaler himself, several rulers from both noble houses would come to ascend and descend the throne several times during their lives.

Of course, a rival royal house was not the only issue that the Draculs had to deal with in their lifetime. It's of vital importance to know that ascending the throne at Târgovişte was somewhat different than, for example, ascending it in Buda at the Hungarian court, or at Constantinople, or anywhere else in the Balkans. Namely, the notion of bastardy didn't really affect who would sit on the throne next. Many of the Wallachian rulers had been born out of wedlock, oftentimes to low-born women. In practice, this meant that literally anyone could ascend to the throne, a practice that had far more setbacks than benefits. For instance, Vlad II himself was an illegitimate child of Mircea, yet he still managed to rule over the country for several years. In addition, he had other children besides his three legitimate sons and one daughter, Alexandra. There was a bastard son named Mircea, on whom we barely have any historical data, and another Vlad who would rule Wallachia on several occasions as Vlad IV Călugărul, or "Vlad the Monk."

Before Vlad II returned to his country, the throne had been seized by a Dăneşti noble, Basarab II, the grandson of Dan I. Basarab had actually enjoyed secret support from John Hunyadi years before Vlad II went to visit the sultan and got captured. After deposing Vlad's oldest son Mircea in 1442, Hunyadi placed Basarab on the throne, but the voivode would only rule for a little over a year. Upon Vlad II's return to Wallachia from the Ottomans, he would swiftly depose the new voivode, although we don't have any reliable data letting us know how he did it. Considering his new treaty with the Ottomans and an already strained relationship with Hungary, we can speculate that the sultan might have helped him in this endeavor. We also know that Basarab II, though deposed, wasn't killed or otherwise harmed by Vlad II, though he would not rise to prominence until his death during the reign of Vlad the Impaler himself.

By the end of 1443, Hunyadi and Władysław III were undertaking their so-called "Long Campaign" against the Ottomans, a crusade that would have devastating results for the Christian forces. In its early stages, the campaign had been successful; the crusaders actually managed to liberate vast areas of Serbian and Bulgarian lands, so much so that even some of their defeats (such as the one at the Battle of Zlatitsa Pass on December 12th, 1443, and the subsequent retreat to Buda) were treated as victories and used as pro-Christian propaganda at the time. Because of these circumstances, Hunyadi and Władysław openly rejected a treaty with the sultan, despite him vehemently pursuing peace talks. Vlad II decided against helping the crusade openly, as did Despot Branković (his daughter Mara, Murad's wife at the time, was actually instrumental in convincing the sultan to sue for peace). Both rulers had heavy ties with the Ottomans, but Vlad II's situation was slightly worse off because of his obligations to the Order of the Dragon, on the one hand, and his young sons being the sultan's prisoners, on the other. Despite trying and failing to convince the crusaders against waging war, he sent a battalion of 4,000 horsemen led by his son, the deposed voivode Mircea II, in 1444. The Polish king Władysław died during the battle, with the Ottomans beheading him and impaling his head on a pike as a display of victory. Hunyadi himself retreated but was subsequently captured by Vlad II and held prisoner for a brief period of time. The reasons behind Vlad's capture of John Hunyadi aren't entirely clear to historians, but he did release him soon after, allowing him to return to Hungary but demanding a large ransom in return.

Vlad II would remain in power until 1447. Several important events took place that further complicated his relations with both the Ottomans and the Hungarians, all of them involving a military campaign between 1445 and late 1446. Assisted by both Hunyadi's forces and a band of crusaders from the Duchy of Burgundy, Dracula's father waged a few successful battles against the Turks, retaking some important forts (such as the one in Giurgiu) and even taking in 11,000 Bulgarian refugees who rebelled against Sultan Murad II. In his final years, Vlad II would return the refugees to the Ottomans and refuse to participate in any other Christian efforts against the overwhelming Muslim force. In late July 1447, Hunyadi openly supported a different pretender to the Wallachian throne, Vladislav II of the Dănești line. The people of Brașov, a city important to both the Transylvanians and the Wallachians, were ordered by Hunyadi to extend their support to the new ruler, and the antagonism for Vlad II grew. Not long after, Hunyadi invaded Târgoviște, the capital of Wallachia. Vlad II managed to flee, but he was captured and killed, more than likely by Vladislav II himself. Vlad's eldest son Mircea was also killed around the same time. In terms of regular rules of primogeniture, Vlad III was, by all rights, the successor to the throne since Mircea had no issue. However, with Wallachia having its own laws regarding the succession, and with the Hungarian general intrusively involved as he was, the throne was anything but secure, no matter who occupied it.

Murad II, painted circa 1800[ii]

Vlad's First Reign (October–November 1448)

Vladislav was the puppet ruler in charge of Wallachia, though, in reality, he had to answer to John Hunyadi. Hunyadi himself might have held direct power over the country for a short while, possibly appointing Vladislav in December as a "legal" successor to the late Vlad II. Strategically speaking, this would have been a savvy move on the Hungarian noble's part; not only would Hunyadi have the loyalty of a ruler whom he had supported for months and reap the material benefits from such an arrangement (in the form of taxes, lands, and privileges), but he would also avoid all the hassle that would come from dealing with the common folk of Wallachia and the members of the nobility, the so-called boyars. It's fascinating to know that the commoners and the members of the nobility, both minor and major, had more of an influence on the current ruling state of affairs than modern history tends to give them credit for. If provoked or unsatisfied, they would rebel, regardless if said rebellions would be fruitful or not. Transylvania and Wallachia, in particular, were notorious for how often the boyars and the commoners of major forts and cities (Târgoviște, Giurgiu, Chilia, Brașov, etc.) would successfully overthrow the ruler they deemed unworthy. It didn't help that various pretenders (legitimate or otherwise, Wallachian/Transylvanian or outsiders) all had different ways of influencing the boyars' opinions directly. Before Vlad III took the throne, the boyars' sense of entitlement and the rebellious attitude of the common folk was such a major issue that even someone as powerful as Hunyadi would end up dead if a few dozen commoners got offended one afternoon. Therefore, appointing a puppet voivode was a way for Hunyadi to avoid all of that hassle and maintain a living head on his shoulders. But there was one more benefit to the general's supposed shifting of the Wallachian throne to Vladislav instead of maintaining it himself. Namely, as a Hungarian noble who had Wallachia's loyalty in the bag, Hunyadi would enjoy major privileges at the court of Buda. By 1446, he had already been appointed regent to the young king Ladislaus V and had been one of the richest barons in Europe, but that didn't stop him from trying to extend his influence further, as he launched several military campaigns in a row, starting with an unsuccessful spat against Ulrich II, Count of Celje. By August 1448, Hunyadi was in a full-on war against the Ottomans, and he wanted to unite his forces with Skanderbeg, the contemporary lord of the Albanian lands and one of the fiercest enemies of the Turks. For the purposes of this unification, Hunyadi took a force of over 16,000 men through Serbia, whose despot remained neutral but was considered a Turkish ally. Vladislav II also contributed to this military effort with 8,000 troops, but more importantly, he himself joined the crusade, leaving the court at Târgoviște wide open. Eventually, Hunyadi would face the Ottomans during the Second Battle of Kosovo in September 1448, which resulted in a catastrophic and humiliating defeat for him. His subsequent capture by the Serbian despot during his retreat from the battle was just another nail in the coffin of this humiliation, though, interestingly enough, even this sequence of events didn't tarnish his reputation significantly with the Christian nations of the Balkans. Even among his contemporaries, the Hungarian baron enjoyed a great deal of respect amongst the Wallachians, the Transylvanians, the Bulgarians, the Serbs, and the people of the Crown he served.

Naturally, all of these events were perfect for Vlad III to step onto the Balkan political scene in 1448. In October, while Hunyadi and Vladislav II were on their way to battle the Ottomans, the young Wallachian voivode in exile returned to his country and, via a bloody coup and with the assistance of the Ottoman forces, took the throne at Târgoviște. By this time, Vlad had proven himself a capable military commander and a leader at heart. As early as his initial stay at Edirne, the young prince was given the rank of an officer within the Turkish army. Sultan Murad II had clearly considered Vlad his preferred choice to take the throne of Wallachia. This was, in large part, due to Vlad's many years of Ottoman "brainwashing"; after all, he had been kept as a prisoner at the royal court and was a valuable hostage, along with his younger brother, to be used as a bargaining chip against Vlad II. But those weren't the only reasons why Murad II (and even Mehmed II during his early reign) favored Vlad. Despite his rebellious behavior against his captors, the youth had proven himself to be cunning and ruthless, just the kind of man to head an army and sit on the throne in the name of the sultan.

It's impossible to know what Vlad had been thinking during this time. Based on his later actions, we can safely say that he had no love for the Turks and that his upbringing at both Eğrigöz and Edirne had been viewed by him as a strategic means to an end—he would learn everything he needed to know about Ottoman battle tactics, and when the time was favorable, and he occupied the throne in Târgoviște, he would use the Turks' own methods of warfare against them. However, as he was alone at the Ottoman court with few real allies, the prince still had to recognize their sovereignty, at least for the time being. During his reclaiming of the throne, Vlad was witness to the Turkish claiming of the fortress of Giurgiu, which would remain under their domain even after his first deposition.

As is more or less expected of medieval Wallachia, Vlad III's first rule barely lasted a month. Though the defeat of the crusaders at Kosovo had been monumental, Vladislav II had managed to survive, as did an unknown but probably significant portion of his army. We can't really estimate the number of the Wallachian survivors, but they must have been sizable since the Dănești voivode managed to reclaim his throne when he returned to Wallachia in November. With his army, Vladislav defeated Dracula's forces, and the new voivode had to flee south of the Danube River. By December 7th, the news of Dracula's deposition had even reached Constantinople; some of the news was clearly false, such as Dracula's death by decapitation or the fact that he had been defeated by Hunyadi rather than Vladislav.

And speaking of both Hunyadi and Vladislav, the end of 1448 saw them both suffer the consequences of their recent actions. Hunyadi's capture by Despot Stefan Lazarević had been a humiliating experience, and it didn't help matters that Vladislav had decided against helping Hunyadi during their retreat from Kosovo (after all, Vladislav had still been in the Serbian lands in October and could have reached the despot in a matter of days). Vladislav's decision to reclaim Wallachia was important politically, but his failure to support Hunyadi had cost him dearly. When Hunyadi was eventually released from the despot's dungeon and returned to Wallachia, he took away two important territories from Vladislav, namely Amlaș and Făgăraș. These settlements had been predominantly Saxon in terms of demographics, but as fiefdoms, they had been the "ancestral home" of the Basarab dynasty, and they were equally important to both branches vying for the Wallachian throne in the late 15th century. By taking them away from Vladislav but still keeping him in power, Hunyadi humiliated the voivode and, at the same time, proved just how much influence he could still exercise even after a major defeat.

Vlad's Exile

Vlad had originally fled to the Ottoman court at Edirne. History doesn't know a whole lot about this brief period, but soon enough, the deposed Wallachian voivode would move again, this time as a guest at the court of Bogdan II of Moldavia. As mentioned earlier, the two lands had always had a form of kinship: both spoke the same language, were largely homogenous in terms of religion, had their royal families intermarry several times, and had provided support for one another during crucial events such as wars, dethronings, and rethronings. And while they didn't always see eye to eye (which we will cover in later chapters), their relations had remained largely stable, even decades after Vlad the Impaler's death.

The deposed voivode had extremely sound personal reasons to find refuge at the Moldavian court. For instance, Bogdan II's sister was his second wife. Bogdan's own wife, Princess Oltea, was of Wallachian origin and probably a member of the Basarab dynasty. She was also the mother of Stephen the Great, who was at Bogdan's court and who would develop a close friendship with Vlad the Impaler. Finally, Bogdan himself had a valid reason to receive Vlad at his court, in what would become the current city of Suceava. During Vlad II's reign, Bogdan had to seek refuge at the court of Târgoviște. The reason behind this event is unknown, but it was more than likely a struggle for the Moldavian throne. Bogdan himself would be assassinated by Petru Aron, the bastard son of Bogdan's father Alexander the Good, in 1451. With a new, hostile ruler on the Moldavian throne, Vlad had to flee again, finding refuge with his father's old enemy, John Hunyadi himself. His plan was for Hunyadi to help him reclaim the throne, which the Hungarian noble would initially refuse to do. However, though his early reign had ended in a series of setbacks, this was merely the beginning for Vlad III. Soon enough, all of Europe would come to know his name.

Chapter 2 – Second Reign: Vlad as a Ruler, Domestic Affairs, Foreign Relations, Wars, Dethroning, and Capture

Most casual history buffs have an idea that some of the best-known monarchs had long reigns that lasted for decades. And while there were people throughout human history that ruled for exceptionally long periods of time, most of them had only a few years of ruling to their name. In fact, some would barely last over a month. Let's be a bit more concrete with this and use the medieval rulers we've mentioned thus far to illustrate the point. Bogdan II of Moldavia, the ally of the Draculs, ruled for a little over two years. Ladislaus V the Posthumous, although he is officially recognized as a ruler from his birth in 1440, didn't actually independently take the throne until 1452, which means he ruled for around five years. And though Vladislav II technically ruled for nine years in total, his first reign (before Dracula seized the throne) was barely a year long. Vlad's own father, Vlad II Dracul, had been a ruler of Wallachia for a grand total of ten years, which was split between two reigns. His predecessor, Alexander I Aldea, had only been a voivode for five years. The son of

Despot Đurađ Branković, Lazar, ruled the despotate after his father for roughly two years and was followed by his cousin Stefan, who only ruled for fourteen months.

With so many examples of brief reigns, which seemed to be as frequent as local wars and uprisings, it's no wonder that Vlad III's longest and most notable period in power lasted a little over six years. When compared to some of the highest-regarded rulers of both Wallachia and Moldavia, such as Mircea I the Elder (ruled for a total of 29 years) and Stephen III of Moldavia, also known as Stephen the Great (ruled for an astounding 47 years), this particular rule of Vlad III seems almost insignificant in comparison. However, it was during these years that Vlad would establish himself as a powerful political player who wasn't afraid of using any means necessary to achieve his goals and bring some stability to his land.

Stephen the Great of Moldavia, Gospel miniature, from the Humor Monastery, 1473

Events that Led to the Second Reign

We don't know the exact course of events that placed Vlad the Impaler back on the throne of Wallachia. However, we can piece together what happened in the few years before he did so. During his exile in Moldavia, Vlad began to repair his relations with the Hungarian Crown; more precisely, he was trying hard to get in the good graces of John Hunyadi.

This wasn't an easy task at the time. The Hungarian kingdom was, effectively, just as hungry for Wallachian territory and influence as the Ottoman Empire. What made them almost a bigger threat than the Turks was their proximity; Wallachia and Hungary were literally neighboring states, while the whole of Bulgaria, Serbia, and what was left of the Eastern Roman Empire stood between Vlad's land and the Ottomans. Moreover, thanks to the efforts of both the current political establishment at Buda as well as the rulers active during Vlad II's time, the Hungarian nobles could lay legitimate claims over large swathes of territory in Wallachia. In addition, they would intermarry and produce offspring that would have hereditary rights over any of the lands. Hungary was effectively in the same position that the Habsburg Monarchy, i.e., the Austrians, would enjoy only a few centuries later.

In one sense, Vlad III was a bit cornered due to this situation with Hungary; outright refusing them would not be an option, as Hunyadi would not only refuse to offer help in case the Ottomans wanted to invade the voivode, but they could also very well attack Wallachia itself. However, Vlad's decision to ally himself with the Hungarian kingdom more closely was actually a prudent political move. Most of his father's Dăneşti-born rivals and claimants to the throne had outside help, and 90 percent of the time, it was the Hungarian king who provided it. Therefore, Vlad would simply use his enemies' tactics against them, and he would do so preemptively.

Despite Vlad's showing of goodwill toward Hunyadi, the Hungarian baron did not immediately (and openly) declare his support right away. After all, Vlad's father was still fresh in the baron's memory, and supporting his hot-blooded, shrewd son might have ended up backfiring on Hungary. There was a general aura of distrust, which was not unwarranted on Hunyadi's part; immediately after taking the throne, Vlad would undertake actions that would do damage to the Hungarian economy and strain their relations even further.

However, Hunyadi himself also proceeded with some steps that would ensure Vlad's mistrust in him. On February 6th, 1452, the baron had instructed the people of Braşov not to shelter Dracula. However, soon after, the Wallachian voivode would return to this city with a task to defend it, a task proclaimed by none other than Hunyadi himself. While we know little of these events, we can safely say, judging by their proximity and outcomes, that the voivode and the baron made peace with one another between 1452 and early 1456.

Wallachia upon Vlad III's Return; Demographic Makeup, Domestic Affairs, Early Issues

The year was 1456, and depending on the source, it was either early spring or mid- to late summer when Vlad III Dracula invaded his homeland of Wallachia and reclaimed the throne from Vladislav II. Some sources even claim that the voivode killed the acting prince himself before declaring his sovereignty. Vlad achieved this victory in no small part thanks to the Hungarian forces sent by Hunyadi. And as a son of a former ruler, he had as much legitimate claim to the throne as the pretenders, some of whom were born bastards and all of whom tried to dethrone the voivode at one point or another. One of these pretenders was Dan III, while another was an unnamed priest mistakenly referred to as Vlad's namesake brother, later known as Vlad the Monk.

Vlad's coronation was not recorded, but based on how some of the later rulers of Wallachia were crowned, we can assume that most of the customs from the past coronations were used in these later ones, albeit with some changes. A typical coronation would involve the presence of all the court dignitaries, members of the clergy, local boyars, and regular folk. The church service itself was held in Church Slavonic, though most of the particularities of the coronation itself were derived from East Roman customs, as was the case with every Orthodox Balkan nation at the time. Typically, a ruler would receive a scepter, a sword, a gold crown with precious gems, the country's standard, its coat of arms, a saber, and a lance. However, judging by the clothes that Vlad wore in the many contemporary descriptions of the voivode, some Ottoman customs must have crept their way into the event. After all, the Impaler's regal clothing had some interesting Ottoman elements to it, including a caftan (a type of robe) made of velvet and silk that the sultans would wear, which was embroidered with gold filaments, buttons made out of precious stones, and fine sable lining.

Naturally, Vlad's coronation and early rule were not without its problems. Just like any ruler at the time, Vlad III needed to have a council. Usually, around twelve people would serve as council members, tending to different duties regarding the court and the state. However, this number is not set in stone, and with scant data on Vlad's reign, we can't know for sure how many members his council(s) ultimately had, nor who they were. Based on what we do know, however, Vlad had the habit of disposing of any council member he deemed unworthy, often in brutal ways.

From 1456 to 1462, we have records of several key people during Vlad's reign. One individual who, at first, hadn't held any real office position during most of Vlad's early childhood and adolescence was an elderly court scholar named Manea Udriște. He held the title of vornic, which would be the equivalent of a supreme judge. This was the same position he held during the reigns of several rulers, but in 1453, his own son Dragomir would succeed him, serving as a vornic to Vladislav II. Because of this circumstance, Vlad III saw Dragomir as a staunch adversary, so vornics disappeared from the political scene altogether during the Impaler's second reign, coming back well after Vlad had been deposed and held captive by the Hungarians.

Of course, Manea was merely the first council member attested by historical documents to have served under the Impaler. Some of the other notable members include:

- Codrea, a vornic in 1457, stationed in Braşov
- Dragomir, son of Ţacal, a high-ranking boyar and possible vornic between 1457 and 1459
- Voico, son of Dobriţa, first counselor between 1457 and 1461
- Stan, son of Negrea, a high-ranking boyar who also served under Vladislav II; his service ended probably around 1459
- Duca (also Doukas), a Greek jupan (or *župan*, a Slavic title with the rough meaning of "grand prince") who also served during Vladislav II's and Radu the Beautiful's reigns, attested only in 1457
- Cazan, son of Sahac, a council member of the Wallachian court since the 1430s, attested as a chancellor in 1457
- Calcea, attested in 1457 as Vlad's secretary, later promoted to chancellor
- Linart (also Leonard or Leonhard), a Transylvanian Saxon from Braşov, attested as Vlad's Latin secretary and promoted to chancellor in 1461
- Iova, attested as a constable in 1457 and a treasurer in 1458

Vlad's reign was infamous for the way he dealt with insubordinate or inefficient council members. Quite a few of the ones listed here disappeared from court documents altogether after less than a year since they were appointed (or at least attested to be in power). That's because Vlad had the habit of executing any high-ranking boyar who didn't perform his duties as prescribed. There were a few exceptions, however. The most notable was Cazan, a man who had been in the court's service since the reign of Alexander Aldea in 1431. More impressive is the fact that he remained a court official until 1478, having been everything from a boyar to a chancellor and even a jupan.

One other key aspect of Vlad's "revolving" council is the fact that some of its members had openly served his enemies, mainly the pretenders from the Dănești line. It would seem that Vlad was wise to execute them since those who were banished or managed to escape later came back to serve Vlad's opponents. Duca is the best example of this phenomenon. Initially being Vladislav II's councilor all the way back in 1451, he didn't resurface until 1457, the first and only year he would serve under Vlad III. Historians speculate whether he was in league with the Saxons of Transylvania and the Hungarians, which would undoubtedly lead Vlad to believe that Duca was working toward deposing him in favor of a more docile pretender-ruler. Considering that Duca had served Vlad's younger brother Radu for almost six years after Vlad's own deposition, the voivode had been right to get rid of him as early as he did.

Somewhat paradoxically, even though Vlad had obvious xenophobic tendencies, which were almost always justified in some way and, lest we forget, not uncommon for contemporary monarchs, his court of "revolving" council members didn't merely consist of Wallachians. We already saw from the official documents that both Greeks and even Saxons could end up in high positions at Dracula's court. Laonikos Chalkokondyles, an Eastern Roman historian, wrote at length about the Balkans in his famed work *The Histories*, written in ten tomes. Regarding Dracula, Chalkokondyles mentions that the voivode had a court where no council member could trust each other due to how devious they all were. In the historian's own words, Vlad would employ Hungarians, Serbs, Turks, and Tartars if they would serve his purposes. It's also highly likely that a few Moldavians held some important positions, considering Vlad's amicable relations with the rulers of this Romanian-speaking realm. It's fascinating to learn that one of history's most arguably chauvinistic rulers had such a diverse court, with their only common trait being how corrupt they were, a trait that ultimately besets any government body, even today.

As stated earlier, one of the major problems that the Wallachian court had to deal with was the shifty nature of the boyars and the rowdiness of the commoners. Vlad's desire to have full control over who got to sit on his council, as well as his swiftness in removing those that would undermine him, resulted in a country that was a bit more uniform than before. Granted, he wouldn't always reward loyalty on the part of his advisors. Codrea, for example, was staunchly loyal to Vlad III, but that didn't stop the voivode from executing him in 1459.

Vlad's Wallachia was a small, largely rural country. Based on certain estimates and educated guesses, it must have had, at most, 400,000 inhabitants. Of those, more than 90 percent lived in villages. There were only seventeen major market cities, of which three would serve as court capitals. The first was Câmpulung, and it would remain a capital from at least 1300 to 1330, which was when it was replaced by Curtea de Argeş. Târgovişte, Vlad III's capital, would rise to prominence in 1408.

Some of the other major cities in Wallachia included:

- Chilia (or Kilia, modern Kiliya in Ukraine)
- Brăila
- Târgul de Floci
- Giurgiu
- Turnu
- Turnu Severin

Interestingly, no city in Wallachia had strongholds like other cities in the medieval Balkans. The few that did would usually be held by the Hungarians or the Turks. Instead, the local populace would choose to hide in forests or monasteries if there was a major war or a disaster. The cities themselves were poorly fortified, with either flimsy brick or wood enclosures around them. To the native Wallachians, that lack of fortification was a blessing in disguise since most fortified cities were constantly fought over by different regional powers; thus, living inside such a city would see a lot more deaths and hold a lot more danger.

Coming back to the population of Wallachia in the Middle Ages, the estimated figures show just how brutal and efficient Dracula's regime had been. When the 1470s came, the same area that was ruled by the Impaler had, at the very least, 60,000 people less than during his time. Of course, wars and uprisings account for some of those losses, but even if we take that into account, the number of people who died during Dracula's reign is staggering.

Within that population, Vlad III actually did have people who were willing to lay down their lives for him, and the majority of them constituted his army. The voivode's troops consisted of two major regiments. The first was the so-called "small army," made up of sons from lesser nobles, certain boyars, and the landowning free folk known as *curteni* (the term being a plural form of *curtean*). There were no more than 10,000 people that made up the small army, which made it merely a third of the larger "great army." This massive regiment consisted mostly of commoners who were old enough to bear arms, and the absolute majority were men.

Medieval seats of the Saxons in Transylvania during the reign of Vlad the Impaler

Vlad III and Foreign Affairs

Vlad and the Hungarians

The Impaler's rise to power bore new challenges and issues. As a voivode, he had to establish or reestablish foreign relations with the surrounding monarchies, including heavyweights such as Hungary and the Ottoman Empire. In terms of the former, Vlad was, at the moment, somewhat safe. John Hunyadi had finally provided open support to him, though it wouldn't last for long, as Hunyadi would soon die in August 1456. However, Hunyadi's word was an important political advantage to Vlad, considering how much influence the baron had had at the court in Buda. With his early death, however, nearly all of the state affairs of Hungary were squarely in the hands of the king, the young Ladislaus V the Posthumous. Vlad immediately set about to swear loyalty to the king, which can be attested from several treaty documents that the voivode signed with the Saxons of both Braşov and Sibiu. These treaties obliged Vlad to defend the Transylvanian Saxons from Turkish invasions and allow the Saxon merchants to move freely without having to pay taxes (though this last privilege was not afforded to the people at Sibiu); in return, the Transylvanians and Hungarians had to provide shelter to the voivode should he be attacked by either an external force or an internal traitor (and with the pretenders to the Wallachian throne emerging on an almost yearly basis, this wasn't an unreasonable request on Vlad's part). Naturally, the Impaler did not uphold his end of the agreement, considering that the Turks were already raiding Transylvania mere days after the signing. It's no wonder, then, that the burghers of Braşov, Sibiu, and Amlaş openly hosted two different pretenders to the throne, Dan and Vlad, respectively, after Hunyadi's eldest son Ladislaus wrote a letter about the Impaler's supposed crimes. After reading the letters, one might get the impression that Ladislaus was purposefully vague in his assessment of the Wallachian voivode, and one would be absolutely right. In the mind of Hunyadi's son, as well as the majority of Hungarian and Saxon nobility in major Transylvanian cities, Vlad was expendable, and they merely needed a good excuse to replace him with someone more submissive.

Of course, Vlad did not earn this treatment out of thin air. At some point between late 1456 and early 1457, the voivode had issued the production of new Wallachian coins. One such coin was the silver *ban*, which was similar to the golden ducats of Vladislav II insofar as it was made out of pure metal and weighed roughly 0.40 grams. Minting coins with their own heraldry and value might seem like a trivial matter, but we need to take into consideration that Hungary and Wallachia had been in a monetary union since 1424. In other words, the Wallachians were under obligation to use Hungarian coins, which made them, in no small part, financially reliant on the Buda court. With their own mint, the Wallachians gained a new level of autonomy, which would harm Hungarian interests. Moreover, the Hungarian coins were dangerously devalued at this time, as opposed to the new ones issued by Vlad III.

The other potential reason why Vlad was deemed an enemy by Ladislaus Hunyadi and the Transylvanians was the fact that he wanted to reclaim old territories that were no longer under direct Wallachian rule. Vlad would launch concentrated attacks on Braşov, Sibiu, and Beckendorf, a town that supposedly housed Dan III, one of the pretenders to the throne during Dracula's reign.

What's more interesting is that Dracula's sieges of Braşov and Sibiu were not entirely for his own benefit. Namely, despite Ladislaus's treatment of him, the voivode remained loyal to the Hunyadis, which would prove to be instrumental in the events to follow. After John Hunyadi's death in August 1456, his older son, along with his widow Elizabeth and his surviving brother-in-law Michael Szilágyi, created a rift in Hungarian court politics. Hunyadi's death came less than three weeks after the famous Siege of Belgrade, where he successfully crushed the Ottoman forces of Sultan Mehmed II, the same man who had crushed Constantinople and ended the Eastern Roman Empire a little over three years before the siege. One of the carryover disputes that had remained after Hunyadi's death was his rivalry with Ulrich of Celje; Ulrich would eventually be killed by Ladislaus Hunyadi on November 9th of the same year. Considering Ulrich's position as one of King Ladislaus V's regents, the young monarch had to swear to the House of Hunyadi that he would not pursue vengeance. However, his loyal barons, among whom were powerful figures such as Ladislaus Garai, Ladislaus Pálóci, and

Nicholas Újlaki, strongly opposed this decision, and the country was flung into a de facto civil war. Garai and Pálóci were high-ranking court officials, with the former being a palatine (something akin to a viceroy or a regent) and the latter being a judge royal, which was the rank directly beneath the palatine. Újlaki, on the other hand, was a voivode of Transylvania, a position he shared with the now-late John Hunyadi, so his involvement in this matter would directly influence matters in Wallachia as well.

The aforementioned barons were merely three of the many supporters of Ladislaus the Posthumous. However, there was a growing sentiment that the House of Hunyadi should take the throne. The idea materialized when Ladislaus V imprisoned both Ladislaus Hunyadi and his younger brother Matthias, having the older brother executed in March of 1457. In retaliation, Elizabeth and Michael Szilágyi would form the so-called Szilágyi – Hunyadi Liga (League), a movement openly supporting the dethronement of Ladislaus and the elevation of young Matthias to the rank of king. Their troops began to raid the Hungarian regions east of the river Tisza, forcing the young king to flee to Vienna and take Matthias with him. While there, Ladislaus the Posthumous died unexpectedly on November 23rd, 1457. He had no issue, so a brief interregnum ensued. In order to avoid a proper civil war and to appease all parties, the Hungarian Diet (equivalent to a modern parliament) crowned Matthias king on January 24th, 1458. He married Anna, the daughter of Ladislaus Garai, who also happened to be the widow of Matthias's late older brother, sealing the treaty between the loyalists and the Liga. In addition, Michael Szilágyi became the regent of the new young king. Interestingly, though Nicholas Újlaki had been one of the biggest opponents of the Hunyadis, he would end up being one of King Matthias's most trusted supporters in later years, earning several important titles. Most of these titles were related to the territories in the West Balkans (he was dubbed the king of Bosnia, which had already been an Ottoman territory at the time, as well as the ban, a high-ranking noble akin to a prince, of Croatia, Slavonia, and

Dalmatia, and, more importantly, a perpetual count of Teočak, an area in Bosnia near today's city of Tuzla). In other words, Újlaki had next to nothing to do with Transylvania long after Vlad III's deposition.

Michael Szilágyi was a key figure in Vlad's reign during 1457. As a loyal Hunyadi supporter, he launched a few campaigns against the Szeklers and the Saxons of Transylvania, focusing on Sibiu and Braşov. He did this in early 1457, around the same time that Vlad III issued his ultimatums to these cities. The Szilágyis and Vlad III took a decisive victory, forcing the local Saxon burghers and the people loyal to Ladislaus V to sign a treaty favoring the winning side. Vlad gained much from this treaty: the pretender Dan was expelled from the area, and the locals were under obligation to refuse any further aid to him. In addition, Vlad reopened trade with their merchants, which would see a boost in the local economy. Of course, the biggest win was the fact that Wallachian merchants finally had full freedom and safety to trade on Transylvanian soil, a feat no predecessor of Vlad's had managed to achieve despite years of failed attempts. In short, the Hungarian power struggle was the perfect opportunity for the Impaler to kill a few birds with one stone: first, to reclaim territories that he saw as his ancestral home (intriguingly, the treaty itself was signed in his native Sighişoara); next, to provide an easy economic boon for his country's merchants with minimal losses on his part; then, to secure a powerful outside ally in the form of Michael Szilágyi and to establish himself as a relevant political factor in the region; and finally, to establish himself as a dominant force in his native Wallachia and as a deterrent against any potential claimants to his throne. Vlad had been in power less than a year, and he had already accomplished this much simply by making prudent, strategic choices.

However, Vlad's good fortune would not last long. King Matthias would dismiss Garai as his palatine and later persuade Szilágyi to renounce his title as regent. In June of 1458, Szilágyi was appointed as the count of the district of Bistriţa, one of several major seats of the Transylvanian Saxons. Though Szilágyi himself didn't resign as regent until the next year, young Matthias was effectively the sole ruler of the kingdom, and the two were immediately at odds. Because of the raven that was featured prominently on the House of Hunyadi's coat of arms, Matthias bore the nickname Corvinus, a sobriquet his issue would inherit.

Unlike some of his predecessors, Corvinus favored the Saxons over the Wallachians, hence why he didn't provide immediate support to Vlad III. In fact, while Szilágyi was plotting against the young king (and was arrested for his actions in Belgrade by the end of the year), Corvinus dispatched an envoy, the Polish noble known as the Benedict of Boythor, to Wallachia to have a delicate discussion with the voivode. According to legend (which we will cover in a later chapter), the ambassador didn't exactly feel welcome at the court in Târgoviște. In fact, he was downright terrified of the Wallachian ruler, and to be fair, if he hadn't approached the matter prudently, he would have most likely been killed on the spot. Benedict's mission was to convince Vlad III to stabilize his relations with the Transylvanian Saxons, who, in turn, would admit to wronging the voivode and his people in the past. Because of his history with the Saxons, Dracula wasn't too pleased with this task set before him by the young king. In fact, he would do the exact opposite in the coming months—not only would he issue a new silver ducat and have it minted in the new capital of Bucureşti, but he would reinstate the trading bans and high taxes to all Saxon merchants from Sibiu and Braşov. To be precise, he limited their capacities to three cities in total: Câmpulung, Târgşor, and Târgoviște. The Wallachians were, once again, exempt from these new laws, clearly letting the Saxons know where they were in the voivode's pecking order.

Vlad III was also asked to join the possible crusade against the Turks. The reasons for these were aplenty: Serbia, a notably weak country at that point, was going through political turmoil after the death of Despot Lazar Branković. His brother, known as Stephen the Blind, and Lazar's widow, Helena Palaiologina, held power and wanted to pledge their allegiance to the Hungarian court. However, an army commander known as Michael Angelović wanted to become a vassal of the Ottomans, largely due to the fact that his own brother, Mahmud Pasha, was the grand vizier and the sultan's main advisor at the time. Lazar's successors arrested Angelović, which prompted Sultan Mehmed II to send Mahmud Pasha with an army to Serbia and finish the conquest. At that point, only the city of Semendria (modern-day Smederevo) managed to withstand the Turkish advances.

The reason why Serbia's inevitable downfall was important to both King Matthias Corvinus and Vlad III is rather pragmatic. The remnants of the Serbian Despotate were literally the only thing that stood in the way between the Ottomans, on one side, and Wallachia and Hungary on the other. Without that buffer, both countries were exposed to potential lootings, attacks, incursions, and other dangers. Luckily, Mahmud Pasha didn't reach Semendria properly; according to some eyewitness accounts, which were written by an anonymous contemporary of these events, the Turkish commander entered Wallachia, claimed a fortress (more than likely the one at Turnu Severin, though this is yet to be confirmed), and, after attempting to cross the Danube with his soldiers and his prisoners, was brutally attacked by Dracula and his army of 5,000 people, which consisted of both Wallachians and Hungarians. If the historical account is to be believed, out of 18,000 Ottoman soldiers, less than 8,000 were able to retreat. The rest were either killed in battle or drowned in the river. The Serbian question would, of course, not be solved properly, as Matthias had agreed in a council with Holy Roman Emperor Frederick III to marry Despot Lazar's daughter to the current king of Bosnia, which was another failing state at the time. In 1459, Mehmed II would finally annex what was left of Serbia, leaving Hungary, Transylvania, and Wallachia exposed to further attacks.

Matthias Corvinus, due to Vlad's actions against the Saxons and the Szeklers, began to provide support to the pretenders to the Wallachian throne, not unlike how his father had handled things back in the day. Two of these pretenders were known as Basarab II and

Dan III, the latter of which was presumably killed by Vlad himself in a particularly gruesome way. In addition to these actions, the young king had also allowed these pretenders to seek shelter among the Transylvanian Saxons, but more importantly, he prohibited any merchants from Braşov to trade arms with the Wallachians.

This animosity between the rulers would last at least up until 1460. However, as the years went by, the two men grew to understand one another, and their relations became somewhat normalized. In fact, in 1461, Matthias proposed that the Wallachian voivode marry a woman from his family, the noblewoman (and Vlad's future second wife) Jusztina Szilágyi. This bit of news greatly unnerved Sultan Mehmed II, who rightfully saw it as a way for Vlad to strengthen his alliances with the other Christian nations and possibly work on a way to fight off the Turks. In the final years of Vlad's second reign, this would spiral into war and deliver heavy losses to both sides.

Relief of King Matthias Corvinus, from Beatrice of Naples and Matthias Corvinus, *author unknown, circa 1485–1490 (this piece is a later copy from the 19th century)*[5]

Vlad and the Turks

Initially, though not willingly, Vlad had been an ally to the Ottomans. For instance, he would not openly attack them during the

43

early months of his reign, opting to stay, more or less, neutral with strengthening only some of the key relations with the Hungarians and the Moldavians. Interestingly, unlike most vassal states during the reigns of Murad II and Mehmed II, Wallachia had remained largely autonomous. Vlad, of course, had to pay an annual tribute to the Turks to prevent the wrath of the sultan's army. However, there were a few key elements that made him a more independent ruler than his contemporaries. For instance, none of Vlad's immediate family members were prisoners of the sultan other than his brother Radu. However, by this point, Radu had been staying at the Ottoman court willingly, having become somewhat of a favorite to the sultans. In fact, it might have even been Radu's insistence that brought Vlad III to the throne in the first place, which is made all the more plausible considering that the Impaler hadn't made any attacks on the Turks in his early reign.

Another important element to Wallachia's autonomy in 1456 was the fact that Vlad, even during the final days of his reign, never sent any young boys as a tribute. Sources from the time attest that he had to send at least 500 young boys to the sultan each year, but based on Vlad's personal correspondence with the rulers at the time (including his letter to King Matthias Corvinus), there didn't seem to be any mention of this demand on the side of the Ottomans. A reader might conclude that Vlad simply lied by omission that he didn't have to send any young boys as a tribute, but this is highly unlikely. After all, he clearly stated in his letters what he believed the Turks were planning and what dangers they posed to his country and countrymen. As someone seeking help against an aggressor, it would be illogical to leave out such a significant method of subjugation as the Devshirme.

We can find the third and final element that proves Vlad hadn't been a completely submissive vassal of the Ottomans within the legal documents from his time. While he was in power, Vlad had refused the Ottomans free passage through Wallachia for the purposes of raiding the Transylvanians. They were also not allowed to settle in Wallachia permanently, buy or own land, construct mosques, or attain any proper political power. In addition, Orthodox Christianity was freely practiced, and the prince, if not by means of primogeniture, could only be elected by the boyars and the clergy, not by the Ottomans directly.

Vlad III's Wars: Major Battles and Campaigns

The Danubian Campaign

Vlad's shaky relations with nearly everyone would soon bear bitter fruit. When Mehmed II learned of the voivode's planned marriage with the cousin of the Hungarian king in early 1462, he sent an envoy to try to convince Vlad to visit the Sublime Porte (the Ottoman's medieval court) and discuss future endeavors. The servant whom the sultan dispatched to finish this task was a Greek secretary known as Thomas Katabolenos, a skilled diplomat recommended by the ecumenical Christian patriarch himself. After the fall of Constantinople, the Greeks, who still considered themselves as Eastern Romans, were under the sultan's rule, but he did not exactly rule over them directly; instead, the patriarch and the Church took over most of the governing duties as proxies. Considering the status of the Eastern Roman Orthodox Church as ecumenical, i.e., the one above all others, the Orthodox Churches of both Wallachia and Moldavia were its direct underlings. Therefore, Mehmed II's move was quite prudent. A diplomat with the knowledge of Christian affairs would be able to convince Vlad more easily to visit the sultan than any Muslim diplomat would.

But Vlad was anything but ignorant of what this invitation meant. His own father had made the mistake of appearing at the sultan's court before, and the whole family ended up in disarray after that, to put it mildly. Therefore, the Impaler asked the sultan to send a local bey (a title meaning "chieftain of an area of land") to "guard the frontier and keep the country safe"; the reasoning Vlad used was, indeed, quite sound and surprisingly accurate, as he claimed that the country, which would be left to the local boyars, would fall apart since nobody was faithful to him. With that in mind, Mehmed II sent Hamza Bey, the governor of Nicopolis, to watch over the Danube River.

Cunningly, Dracula sent a letter to King Matthias Corvinus, warning him of the dangers that the Turks posed and, almost predictably, stating that his venture into Constantinople would mean his death and that Hamza Bey was more than willing to drag Dracula to the Ottoman's new capital, by force if necessary. So, Dracula acted quickly, capturing both Hamza Bey and Thomas Katabolenos and impaling them soon after. Around forty of their men were also impaled and mutilated, with their corpses lining the walls of Târgoviște.

Of course, that was merely the precursor to what we call Dracula's Danubian campaign. Not long after he had the two servants of the sultan dispatched, Vlad took his army across the frozen Danube and divided the men up into several squads. His plan was to cover all of the frontier lands next to the great river, from Chilia in the southeast to Rahova in the northwest, near the mouth of the Jiu River. It was a massive 800-kilometer (almost 500-mile) swath of land to cover, and they had to do this in the midst of a devastating winter, no less. But Vlad III did far more than simply succeed in his intended mission. In fact, he utterly crushed nearly everything next to the Danube River that wasn't Wallachian. In the process, he recaptured the important fortress of Giurgiu, reportedly ordering the locals to open the gates in fluent Turkish before having his men flood it and murder anything that moved.

Both Turks and local Bulgarians died in the constant raids, killed either on land or while on the river transporting goods. No women or children were spared during this horrific raid, and all of the people that didn't die by the sword would succumb to the flames of one of the hundreds of fires. By his own estimate, which might be exaggerated but is fascinating nonetheless, the voivode claims to have killed a grand total of 22,883 people. And, in his own words, those were just the ones whose heads were accounted for. He didn't count any of the people burned alive or killed in such a way that you couldn't separate the head from the body.

Aside from this mass murder, tantamount to genocide if not for the diverse nationalities that died under Wallachian swords, Vlad also ordered the destruction of material goods, transport vehicles like carts and rafts, houses, keeps, churches, and what few forts there were on the Danube on the Bulgarian side. His plan was to completely cripple the locals from funding and supplying the Ottoman troops in case the sultan felt like invading the voivode. But more importantly, Vlad wanted to show the Turks that he meant business, that even the best-prepared armies of the sultan could do no damage to his own warriors, and that he was both capable and willing to murder thousands of civilians to prove his point.

In a lengthy letter he sent to King Matthias Corvinus, Vlad lists off all of the cities, towns, villages, and forts that ended up burned, sacked, or damaged after he laid his siege. There is no real sympathy in the voivode's voice for all of the innocents that died; he merely lists them off and brushes them aside in the very next sentence. What's more disturbing, however, is the duplicity of some of Vlad's statements. He claims to have done what he did for the preservation of Christianity, the Catholic faith, and the crown of the Hungarian king, but every single one of those statements is patently hypocritical. Based on every source we have, Vlad only converted to Catholicism during his imprisonment, which took place sometime before his death. Up until that point, he was more than likely an Orthodox ruler, even if he wasn't practicing and despite his heinous acts while at court. Next, we know that he rarely put stock in Christianity as a moral goal, considering that he had refused to join a few potential crusades. Moreover, the Hungarian crown didn't exactly mean much to him, other than the fact that it was placed on the head of a powerful political ally (whose position at court was, at best, as shaky as his own in Wallachia). And lastly, Vlad had committed most of these atrocities against innocent Christian men and women of Bulgaria. No self-described fighter for Christianity would even think to condone the murder of civilians, let alone in the way that Vlad had done it.

The Night Attack

With the letter sent, it was Corvinus's time to act. Thanks to his efforts, this same letter reached other European rulers at the time, even finding its way to northern Italy. Though Matthias might have felt sympathetic to Vlad's cause (or at least saw an opportunity to crush the Ottomans), his royal budget and the state of his court would not allow him to waste any money on an anti-Turk campaign. He lobbied hard with various Italian nobles and the clergy for monetary assistance in this potential crusade, but it ultimately came to nothing. Alone, Corvinus could simply not risk a war with the sultan.

The defeat of the Ottomans was so crushing and devastating that it's not a stretch to call it their biggest defeat (up to that point) since Mehmed II came to power. Naturally, the Porte had to retaliate, so the sultan amassed what was possibly the biggest army since the Siege of Constantinople, which had taken place less than a decade prior. Two of the main regiments of his army consisted of ground troops, with himself at the helm. They headed directly for Dracula's old capital of Târgoviște. The fleet, however, was in Brăila, a port city close to another important inhabited area, the contested city of Chilia. Stephen the Great of Moldavia had always been an ally to the Wallachian voivode, but Chilia never stopped being a hot-button issue, one that the Moldavian ruler sought to fix. Brăila itself would be burned to the ground, but Chilia would not fall into Ottoman hands, nor would it go back to Prince Stephen that year. Though the Turks themselves saw this port as extremely important and placed great emphasis on capturing it, they wouldn't seize control of it until 1484.

Vlad had seen the sizable army of Mehmed II. On June 4th, 1462, the army crossed the Danube at Nicopolis (modern Nikopol in Bulgaria) and moved steadily toward Târgoviște. Once again showing his cunning nature, Vlad employed a scorched-earth policy; every time he retreated, his army would burn the crops and destroy all the dwellings, leaving nothing but ash to the conquerors. The hot summer sun greatly helped Vlad in this endeavor. By the end of the campaign, the Turkish troops had suffered great heat exhaustion and strokes, with the losses on their side being significantly higher than those on the Wallachian side. However, Vlad's real moment of triumph, as well as potentially his biggest failure, would come on the night between June 17th and June 18th.

Several different historical accounts at the time spoke of this attack, and while there are some significant variations in terms of details, the basic course of events is the same. Upon reaching Târgoviște but before entering it, the Ottomans set up a base camp. Vlad saw this as a great opportunity for a task that was nowhere near easy but which could change the course of the war significantly. Taking anywhere between 7,000 and 10,000 men, the voivode divided them into two groups and attacked the camp at night, when the Ottomans least suspected it. His main goal was to kill Mehmed II and his chief viziers. The murders of these individuals would then act as a catalyst for the Turkish armies to fall into disarray. Had Vlad succeeded, there would have been a dynastic battle at the Porte, allowing the Christian nations of the Balkans to breathe a sigh of relief for a short while and reorganize their efforts. Sadly, Vlad did not harm the sultan (though, according to some sources, the voivode's army did wound Mehmed, albeit not fatally) and had to retreat into the thick Wallachian woodland. The Ottomans were, reportedly, terrified beyond belief, and after the confusion had settled, they somehow managed to capture a number of Wallachian soldiers and decapitate them in retaliation.

Vlad's final proper act of defiance was caused by his absence from Târgoviște when the Ottomans reached it by the end of June. Sources claim that the Muslim army had entered a deserted town, which was littered with impaled corpses of all ages, both male and female, and all nationalities. They even recognized some of the court dignitaries from Constantinople that had been dispatched earlier that year. The sultan himself stated that he could not deprive Wallachia of such a cruel yet competent ruler, so he left the capital, with his men dumbfounded and confused as to what had just happened.

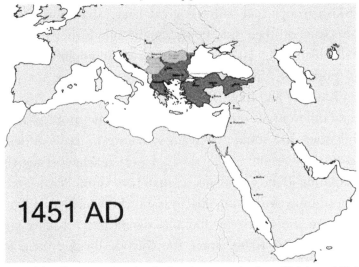

Map of the Ottoman Empire during the second reign of Mehmed II the Conqueror; Wallachia and Serbia shown in light-green[iii]

Final Battles of 1462 before the Dethroning

Upon his retreat, Mehmed began his movement toward Chilia, which was now under attack from Stephen the Great. Some documents from this time imply that the Moldavian prince had begun raiding Vlad's borderlands earlier that year, even as early as before Mehmed's campaign. Considering the friendship and alliance between the two rulers (both before and after 1462), this action on the part of Stephen might seem confusing at first until we talk more about the city of Chilia.

As an important port, it had been in the hands of the Wallachians (or rather the Hungarians through a Wallachian proxy) since 1448. Stephen saw an opportunity to reclaim it in the summer of 1462 when it was garrisoned by a mix of both Hungarian and Wallachian troops. But in order to do that, he needed to find the right moment, so he agitated Vlad in order to split his attention between the Moldavian troops and the approaching Turks. Once the Turks had returned from the Wallachian lands, the Moldavian prince laid siege to the city.

It's not impossible to think that Stephen managed to convince the Ottomans that they were allies due to his actions against Vlad, and even contemporary historians like Chalkokondyles and Tursun Bey, Mehmed's own secretary, claim that Stephen had been loyal to the sultan. However, the siege of this city was a failure for the attackers. Not only would the Ottomans suffer yet another defeat at the hands of the Wallachians, but Stephen himself was also wounded in his left ankle, an injury that never properly healed and which was the primary cause for the gangrene infection that killed the Moldavian prince in 1504.

Vlad himself had also started moving toward Chilia, leaving roughly 6,000 soldiers to defend the realm from the Ottomans, which they failed to do. Not long after, another pretender to the throne appeared in the Bărăgan Plain, a vast area extremely close to Târgovişte and a fertile land that housed some of Wallachia's biggest cities at the time. During his campaign, Mehmed II had taken with him a familiar servant who was his favorite in every way. Upon arriving in Wallachia, Radu the Handsome began to campaign hard in order to get as many boyars to accept him as the ruler and avoid more Ottoman attacks. Within months, the two brothers would clash in battle several times, and nearly all of those battles were won by Vlad. Nevertheless, more and more boyars began defecting to Radu, and the Ottoman forces did not stop advancing, leaving Vlad with barely any allies in his crucial moments.

Historians from mid-20th century Romania almost exclusively claimed that Vlad had done nothing but win against the Ottomans and that his exclusion from the throne was solely due to the traitors among the boyars. Of course, a more nuanced view suggests that there were a myriad of reasons. While it is absolutely true that there were boyars defecting to Radu, the number of potential traitors had greatly decreased while Vlad was in power, thanks in no small part to his brutal way of dealing with those who opposed him.

Dethroning and Capture of Vlad the Impaler

Stephen the Great's armies were now an enemy. The Ottomans did not slow their march. Towns and cities burned all over. Radu had become the voice of a significant number of traitorous boyars. All of those elements together were slowly but surely leading to Vlad's downfall in late 1462. An opportunist as always, Vlad retreated to the Carpathian Mountains, effectively dethroning himself and giving Radu all of the power. The voivode's plan was to meet up with Matthias Corvinus and, with the help of the Hungarians, reestablish his rule. But the situation kept getting grimmer by the day. Albert of Istenmező, a Szekler count at the time, declared that the Transylvanian Saxons were going to shift their allegiance to Radu and recognize him as the new voivode. In addition, the younger Dracul also struck up a deal with the Saxons of Brașov, promising them financial and economic benefits in exchange for their loyalty.

The young Hungarian king had, on the surface level, taken Vlad's pleas for help into consideration, seeing as he was in Transylvania in November 1462. Stephen the Great's stance on waging war against the Turks did not change from earlier that year, though—he simply did not have the manpower, nor the money, to finance the endeavor. The two rulers negotiated for weeks before the meeting, it would seem, but judging by what happened (and the documents that surfaced later), we can safely assume that Corvinus had absolutely zero intention of assisting Vlad. He ordered his mercenary commander, a Czech strategist called John Jiskra of Brandýs, to capture Vlad, which Jiskra did near the town of Rucăr. Some accounts state that it was Vlad's own companions who rebelled and captured him at the fortress of Piatra Craiului and then handed him over to Jiskra. Other sources state that Vlad was captured on his way back to Wallachia after the negotiations with the Hungarian king fell through.

Historians do not know the reason behind Corvinus's capture of Vlad in 1462. Even Corvinus's court historian, an Italian poet and famed humanist Antonio Bonfini, states that he did not know why the king captured the voivode. There are three important documents that relate directly to this event, and they were sent to both Pope Pious II in Rome and to the Venetians, who had actually sent some money to finance a potential crusade against the Ottomans during Vlad's military exploits. These documents are the supposed letters that Vlad himself had written. One of them was meant for Sultan Mehmed II, the other for his grand vizier Mahmud Pasha, and the third for Stephen the Great of Moldavia. Apparently, they all contain the same basic premise, with the voivode promising to invade Hungary if the Turks helped him stay in power.

After analyzing these letters, we can safely say that they are forgeries. Dating them reveals that they were most likely written during Vlad's captivity in the Hungarian town of Visegrád. More importantly, by analyzing the style and sentence structure, we can definitely conclude that none of Vlad's character, which emanates from letters that actually came from him, is present. These letters were, therefore, made to justify Vlad's imprisonment to King Matthias's Catholic allies from across the Adriatic, though we may never know why exactly the voivode was captured in the first place.

Chapter 3 – Final Years: A Decade and a Half of Captivity, Third Reign, Death

Vlad's Captivity in Hungary

In late 1462, Vlad was held at "Belgrade," though not the one that served as the former capital of medieval Serbia but rather a town in Wallachia (now named Alba Iulia). Soon after, however, he would be moved to Visegrád and would remain there for the better part of the next fourteen years

Very little is known about Vlad's captivity at Visegrád since there are no reliable records that tell us how he behaved or how he was treated, other than a few legends of him supposedly butchering a woman and exposing her womb simply to show that he did not impregnate her with his bastard child. However, based on what little information we do have on Dracula from the final few years of his life, we can piece together a possible chain of events.

Due to Jiskra's profession, it's not unlikely to think that the mercenary's own men were in charge of being Dracula's jailors. After his transfer from Alba Iulia to Visegrád, Vlad must have only been treated as a prisoner for a short while, long enough for the news of his capture and his cruel nature to reach the wider population of Europe. It's generally thought that the original incunabula (plural of incunabulum, meaning "book" but more specifically referring to pamphlets printed before 1501) that told the story of the voivode's brutalities were printed in Vienna in around 1463, possibly by an individual named Ulrich Han. And though the original text has been lost to time, at least four different copies have survived to this day, all kept at various locations in Austria, Switzerland, France, and the United Kingdom. The pamphlets about Vlad the Impaler must have been quite popular at the time, considering how many copies were made. Whether they reached the court at Buda is not known, though experts suggest that King Matthias Corvinus himself must have been at least aware of them. More importantly, whether or not Vlad himself saw the pamphlets is an unanswered question, but judging by his overall character, he would have probably not cared for their contents.

Historians debate whether Vlad remained at Visegrád or moved to Pest at some point. What we do know is that he owned a house in Pest, implying that even in captivity, he was able to own property within the borders of Corvinus's kingdom. If we apply this assumption on a larger scale, we realize that Vlad was not a mere prisoner. He was, in fact, probably treated more like a high-ranking noble and a "guest of honor," albeit obviously less pompous. He would also buy a house in Pécs, a home that is currently known as the *Drakula háza* ("the House of Dracula"). His widow, Jusztina Szilágyi, would end up inheriting this home after the voivode's death.

In the summer of 1475, after a long six months of beating back the Turks in the Battle of Vaslui and dethroning Radu the Handsome, but shortly after helping place the pretender Basarab Laiotă on the throne of Wallachia for the fourth time, Stephen the Great of Moldavia wrote to the Hungarian king, urging him to release Vlad and recognize him as the legitimate ruler over his native land. And while King Matthias did release Vlad that year (which was the same year Vlad would marry Jusztina and apparently convert to Catholicism), he did not provide the voivode with any troops against the invading Turks and the traitorous Basarab, who was, at the time, allied with Sultan Mehmed II against the Moldavian forces. It is this period, between the end of 1475 and the end of 1476, that we have the most information about the Impaler's exploits, which all took place before his third reign and eventual death.

Castle of Visegrád, a contemporary woodcut during the reign of Matthias Corvinus, 1480[iii]

Military Exploits in Bosnia

At some point in early 1476, possibly late January, King Matthias ordered some of his most reliable noblemen to take up arms against important forts in Bosnia and near its borders in order to expel the Ottomans. Both Vlad III and the Serbian noble Vuk Grgurević (a member of the House of Branković) set off to help with the siege of Šabac, now a modern-day city in Serbia but an important fort back then. The siege was long and drawn out, possibly lasting for a month and a half until the two expatriate nobles took a decisive victory with the Turks surrendering.

Having won this war, the two princes moved to besiege Srebrenica; however, they did so using entirely different tactics. They sent a total of 150 men disguised as Turks into the town so that they could intermingle. Vlad and Vuk, along with the bulk of the army, which was some 2,000 men strong, traveled at night so as not to be spotted. Within days, they seized control of the city, both from the outside and from within, looting and pillaging everything along the way.

Their next major campaign was at the town of Kušlat, which was again won by the Christian forces. The fourth and final victory, however, would come at a cost. While besieging Zvornik, Vuk Grgurević sustained a terrible foot injury during the battle. But the historians of the time paint a far more gruesome picture when talking about Dracula. In their words, he would grab the surrendered Ottomans with his bare hands and rip them apart, flesh, skin, and sinew. He would then proceed to do what he evidently did best, which was impaling them on stakes and leaving them out in the open for everyone to see. Much like in Târgoviște a decade prior, the arriving Ottomans would have been horrified beyond belief at the sight.

Moldavian-Turkish Conflicts of August 1476 and the Retaking of Wallachia

With this string of successes, it was only a matter of time before Vlad and Vuk Grgurević went on to help Stephen the Great flush the Ottomans out of his country. Apparently, they were also joined by a member of the Serbian House of Jakšić, though his name is unknown and is merely assumed to be Demetar. Stephen lost the crucial Battle of Valea Albă in July and was forced to retreat. However, this was a Pyrrhic victory for the Ottomans since they could not capture any of the important Moldavian strongholds, had suffered starvation, and were heavily exhausted by constant small-scale guerilla-style attacks by the local Moldavians. Moreover, there was an outbreak of the plague, which greatly hampered the progress of the Turks.

In August of 1476, Vlad III and the two Serbian nobles were deep within Transylvania, joining forces with the contemporary Transylvanian voivode Stephen V Báthory and his army of 30,000 men. The Christian forces managed to stop the Turkish siege of the fortress at Târgu Neamț and force the Ottomans to flee. Not long after, the Hungarian king issued an order to the Transylvanian Saxons. They were to support Báthory's plan to invade Wallachia in September, which he did, liberating several key cities as he went about his campaign. A mere month later, Vlad the Impaler was in Brașov, reinstating the old trading privileges to the local merchants. Although the Brașov Saxons were still not entirely loyal to Vlad, they began openly supporting him over Basarab Laiotă as early as the first few skirmishes between Moldavia and Wallachia.

Third Reign and Death

November would prove to be the Impaler's glorious return to the throne. During his campaign, Báthory liberated Vlad's old capital, Târgoviște, around November 8th. Vlad himself was in that battle, reportedly defeating Laiotă and causing over 10,000 casualties during the siege. Eight days later, Laiotă's capital of Bucharest also fell, and the voivode, who had been dethroned for the fourth (yet not the final) time, fled to the Ottomans, seeking protection. Vlad and Stephen the Great ceremoniously entered the capital, possibly welcomed by the same disloyal boyars who had, at some point, been betraying nearly every ruler until Vlad's return.

With Vlad's victory, it was the right time to honor his word with the Saxons of Brașov, so the voivode sent the word about his victory to them, urging them to reenter Wallachia and resume their trade. Exactly ten days later, on November 26th, Vlad III Dracula was, yet again, crowned the voivode of Wallachia.

However, this dominion over his country wouldn't last past the end of the year. Prudently, Vlad asked Stephen to leave a contingent of loyal guards to safeguard him. The reason behind this decision was, as it normally tended to be in medieval Wallachia, the inherent distrust of the ruler toward his boyars. After all, those same boyars had, until recently, supported Basarab, and not long before him, they were answering to Vlad's own brother and Ottoman sympathizer Radu the

Handsome. Stephen understood the situation well, leaving Dracula with 200 of his own guardsmen. In December, Laiotă would try to invade Wallachia yet again, this time with a sizable Turkish army backing him. Though accounts greatly differ on the details, we can say for sure that Dracula died fighting, causing heavy losses to the invading force but losing all 200 of his loyal guards in the process. After his death, he was decapitated, and his head was stuffed and sent to Mehmed II in Istanbul. Reportedly, it was paraded around the city for days in celebration of the voivode's final defeat. Stephen the Great received the news of his ally's demise in January of 1477, while the royal court of Matthias Corvinus learned of it a month later. Decades later, Tursun Bey would write about the death of the voivode, calling him *Kazıklı Voyvoda*, which quite literally translates to "impaler lord." The sobriquet was just descriptive and accurate enough to stick, to the point where even later Wallachian rulers would refer to Vlad with this new title. Therefore, Vlad III was never called "Impaler" during his lifetime.

Vlad III Dracula was definitely buried in a monastery, as was the custom of Eastern Orthodox Christian rulers in the Balkans. However, historians still debate as to where his final resting place might have been. The most likely candidate is the Monastery of Snagov since it is also thought to contain the remains of previous monarchs from the Drăculeşti line, including his own father and older brother. However, other experts claim that Dracula would more likely have been buried in the Comana Monastery since he had founded and built it. A headless corpse was found buried near the monastery, suggesting not only that these were Vlad's remains but also that he had breathed his final breath here during the battle.

Chapter 4 – Spreading the Story: Myths about Dracula and His Public Image, Portraits, and Depictions

Even during his lifetime, Vlad the Impaler had been a conversation starter in many European courts. Granted, he wouldn't get the sobriquet "Impaler" until after his death, but even though his name and title were not that ominous, his actions certainly were.

Since the very beginning of his rule, different legends had been popping up all over the medieval world. Considering his strained relations with some nations (and somewhat amicable relations with others), it's only fitting that the negative stereotypes usually associated with Vlad III almost exclusively originated from extremely biased sources. For instance, the Saxons who managed to flee from Transylvania and avoid Dracula's direct field of influence, often settling in other Germanic areas such as the Habsburg Monarchy (precursor to modern-day Austria), began printing various pamphlets retelling stories of the Wallachian ruler's supposed cruelties. On the other hand, Slavic and Wallachian sources present Vlad as a prudent, proactive ruler who took charge of the situation and did what needed to be done. Naturally, both of these sides were essentially printing propaganda that went one way or the other, and more often than not, it amounted to "popular literature." Indeed, a valid point can be made that the incunabula were reprinted by the Saxons in Vienna and other Germanic cities over and over again due to their popularity. After all, even the medieval man loved political scandals, and few can be as interesting as tales of a man who impales his prisoners and tortures them in the worst ways possible.

But how much truth is there to them? Well, oddly enough, even Slavic sources, like the famous *Skazanie o Drakule voivode* ("The Tale of Voivode Dracula"), which are generally more lenient toward the voivode, list off some of his cruel deeds. Of course, these sources, be it positive or negative propaganda, can be trusted wholly on face value. However, we can still look at the basic, bare-bones elements of each contemporary source and come up with some plausible theories.

Let's take impaling, for example. Nearly all propagandistic sources mention Vlad applying this type of punishment in practice. Some state that he did it with the bodies hanging upside down or right side up, others mention mass impalements, and others talk about the way the stake was inserted into the body (or the body rammed onto the stake), etc. Of course, we can't take the numbers of victims given by the ancient authors as gospel since, more often than not, even the most scholarly of medieval writers would exaggerate numbers. So, how do we go about this then? Well, since all sources mention him using impalement as a punishment, we can safely assume that he did so regularly. We also know for a fact that the Ottomans had been using this method of execution for centuries before invading the Balkans, and they were far from being the first to do so. Therefore, even if we reduce the number of victims and decide on the most prominent method, we can claim, without a doubt, that Vlad impaled his adversaries. With that knowledge, the sobriquet "Impaler" is still considered a historical fact, as well as a correct depiction of the man.

Next, we ought to discuss his appearance. We will cover the specific image(s) of Dracula in a little bit, but we do need to find some solid middle ground, just like in our assessment about his propensity for impaling. We know from some of the remaining paintings of the era what Dracula looked like. In other words, there's an actual realistic portrait of the man that we can point to and say, "That, there, is Vlad III." However, we can only be sure about our assessment completely when we look at the Saxon incunabula mentioned earlier. They contain stylized images of Dracula going about his day, and they are quite animated when it comes to movement and gestures. And based on what Vlad looked like in some of these incunabula, he definitely matches the aforementioned realistic portraits prominent in the Late Middle Ages and early Renaissance.

Dracula, like most historical figures of that era (and a huge number of other historical figures from entire millennia before Vlad's birth), is mentioned in very few contemporary documents in a way that gives us a glimpse of his character. That's why historians and researchers have delved deeper into the many legends and myths ascribed to the voivode. As we saw, these sources don't necessarily have to be 100 percent true, but they do give us some good insight into the general image of Vlad III. But the value of these myths goes beyond assessing historical accuracy. They are also splendid works of fiction, tales that have their own meanings and morals, and, in a way, they paint a good picture of what Wallachian (and Southern European) life must have been like when Vlad seized power.

Myths about Vlad III

Over the centuries, plenty of tales have emerged about Vlad's brutal behavior and his blood-sodden habits. Most Western readers have never heard of these legends, which is somewhat disappointing because they can pretty much rival Bram Stoker's novel when it comes to cruelty and gore. This chapter will provide some of these legends, retold in no particular order, chronological or otherwise. Most of them originate from contemporary amateur historians or Saxon booklets printed some years after Vlad's deposition and eventual death. It's also instructive to note that some of these tales have several variations depending on where they were recorded and by whom. Moreover, this is nowhere near an exhaustive list of legends and stories about Vlad III. For instance, no tale that came from rural Romanian folklore is on this list, as those are far too many and, in all likelihood, were crafted well after the voivode's death.

The Bloody Easter

It was March 25th, 1459, Easter Sunday. Matthias Corvinus had become more involved with his kingly duties, the Turks were restless, and there was a lot of commotion in and around Wallachia. Vlad had plenty of problems to deal with: the Saxons of Transylvania wanted to keep the lands of Amlaş and Făgăraş, the ancestral land of the Basarabs, and the young Hungarian king wanted the Wallachians to make peace with the Saxon folk. Of course, Vlad knew what happens when the Hungarian king doesn't support your side and advocates for the benefit of your enemies. He knew it well, considering how many princes and voivodes came before him.

It was on this fateful Easter that he summoned all of his boyars and other members of the nobility for a meal. Nearly 500 of them appeared. Some were as old as oak trees, others barely fifteen of age. Three were boyars he recognized, though a lot more were surely unknown to him. There were even some boyars he wished he didn't know at all. But they were all there, and they ate dinner in reverence of Christ's resurrection.

Soon enough, the meal was done, stomachs were full. The boyars were enjoying a bit of respite from the meal. Ever vigilant, Vlad turned to one of the oldest lords in the keep. "Tell me," he asked the old man, "how many lords and voivodes do you remember who ruled this land before me?" The lord gave his answer. Then Vlad turned to a younger lord and asked the same question. And the young boyar gave his answer. Again, Vlad turned to the next lord, and his answer followed. One by one, Vlad asked them all the same question, and the responses varied greatly. Some lords said, "About thirty, my lord."

Others replied with, "I think twelve, my liege." Some of them would say ten or twelve or twenty, while others would go as high as thirty, forty, and even fifty. Not a single one of the young lords uttered a number smaller than seven.

Satisfied with his answers, Vlad got up from his seat and gave an order to his royal guard. Within minutes, hundreds of screams filled the room as the guards began dragging the boyars out. One by one, the lords and nobles that had dined at Dracula's table were now dying, impaled onto stakes and bleeding profusely to death. It was not unlike a canopy of corpses in front of the royal palace. Many died that day, but many more learned that Vlad didn't think highly of the frequent changes of the voivodes. Indeed, he intended to keep his seat as long as possible, via any means.

The Death of Dan III

Dan III was a pretender to Dracula's throne. He was living in Brașov and enjoying the hospitality of the local Saxon burghers, establishing himself as the anti-voivode to the Impaler. 1459 was coming to a close, and Vlad had already attained the reputation of being a ruthless yet effective ruler. But Dan wasn't afraid. He had the backing of the Hungarian Diet and the king himself. And so, he went about ruling Brașov, issuing a charter here, an edict there. Although he was self-stylized as the lord of Amlaș and Făgăraș, his ambitions went higher. He wanted to be yet another in the long line of revolving princes that occupied the throne of Wallachia. And in order to do that, he would have to go through Vlad.

It was winter, and Dan III had successfully rallied the Saxons. But then again, they didn't need much rallying. Not long ago, their merchants had been forbidden from trading in most of the territory of Wallachia, and the taxes coming from the voivode were dreadful. In addition, information regarding his legendary brutal behavior had reached them mere months prior. Dan knew this information well, and more importantly, he knew how to use it. After all, who would the Saxons support? A man neither loyal to the Crown of Hungary nor the Sultan over at Constantinople? Or the man who openly stood against this tyrant and, more importantly, treated the Saxons with admiration and respect? The local boyars were of one mind—Vlad had to go.

But Vlad didn't budge. The pretender's army crossed the frontier during Easter Week on April 13th, 1460, and went to war with Vlad, a war that Dan lost in the most humiliating way possible. All of Dan's soldiers were captured and executed by April 22nd of the same year, a mere nine days after the incursion had started. Some even reported that Vlad had ordered Saxon women and other women sympathetic to Dan III's cause to be impaled upon stakes as well. Horrifyingly, the babies and infants of these women were also killed and sewn to the dead women's breasts. A truly dreadful sight, to be sure.

But by far, the biggest humiliation came to Dan himself. After he was captured and imprisoned, he was then taken out of his dungeon and brought before the executioners. Vlad himself was there, as were the priests and some of the loyal boyars. But most disturbingly, there lay a gravesite. A gravesite with a tombstone. And it bore Dan's own name on it. The pretender was swiftly placed next to the grave, on his knees, probably too stunned to move. Vlad ordered the priests to read a funeral service for the "late" pretender voivode while some freemen dug a man-sized hole in front of the monument. The only respite Dan could have had was his lack of knowledge of Church Slavonic, the language which the priests were using when reciting their morbid lines. But Dan didn't have to wait long. After the service ended and the priests uttered their last few lines, Vlad had Dan killed on the spot, via decapitation. Whether he did it himself or not, we do not know. But he did deal Dan and all other future pretenders to the throne a crushing blow with a clear message: anyone who tried to take his throne through less than reputable means would find themselves dead.

The Golden Cup

Târgoviște, Vlad's first capital, was quite large, boasting close to 60,000 souls. It had been unruly during the reigns of the previous Wallachian rulers, including Vlad's namesake father and older brother Mircea. The restless and fickle boyars were one reason, but the common folk were no better. Thievery and muggings were common in the capital, as it had an astounding number of poor inhabitants who had to steal to survive, but there were also opportunistic thieves who managed to get away one too many times. But when Vlad came to power, nearly all the criminals in the land started receiving brutal punishments for their deeds. People wouldn't believe some of the stories that merchants and travelers would tell after passing through the voivode's land. Two tales, in particular, stood out.

According to the first tale, a traveler or a merchant had entered Târgoviște and needed a room at an inn to spend the night. However, he was carrying with him large sums of money, which he understandably wanted to deposit somewhere safe. However, the innkeeper and the locals simply told him to keep the money outside with his horse, out in the open. The traveler was stunned, and against his better judgment, he listened to the people and left the bags with his horse. The next morning, expecting to wake up penniless, the traveler was stunned to see the bags intact, with not a single coin missing.

The other tale concerns a certain golden cup. This magnificent dish was placed by Vlad in the middle of Târgoviște's town square. According to his decree, everyone could drink water from this valuable cup. However, if a person was to try and take the cup with them, they would face severe punishment. Vlad ruled Wallachia for six years, and during those six years, not a single soul in his capital city of 60,000 people took the cup.

So, be it the gold of a stranger or a drinking cup for the masses, it was safe on Vlad's streets. People would remember the early days of his rule when thieves still robbed the weak and the powerless. But thanks to Vlad's unusual and disturbing practice of impalement, thieves thought better than to harass people with potentially deep pockets.

A Hearty Meal

Vlad's reputation had already begun to precede him. The king of Hungary knew of his repute, so he sent a total of 55 ambassadors to Dracula's court. The voivode received them well enough, giving them lodgings for the night, as well as food and entertainment. However, he had ordered that stakes be placed, erect, in front of the rooms of each individual ambassador. They were naturally afraid of this development, so they asked the monarch why he did this. He merely stated that it was for his own safety, that he was afraid of treachery. While they were staying at his court, the voivode invaded the Bârsa region. He would proceed to destroy everything—village huts, forts, fields full of wheat and rye, stored grain, it all went up in flames. His men captured the people of the Saxon town of Braşov, which allowed the dreaded prince to reach into the city as far as the chapel of St. Jakob. Before he arrived, he issued orders to have the town's suburbs burned to a crisp, which his men did, allowing the smoke and ash to welcome the ruler into the city.

But the Wallachian monarch didn't rest. The very next morning, he ordered the prisoners to be taken outside. Each and every prisoner was lined up at the foot of the mountain where the church of St. Jakob rested. The prisoners were many and varied: old men and women alike, youths not older than five, men and women of all statures and standings—all of them were now his prisoners. Of course, as was his wont, Vlad ordered a mass execution by impalement. Every single prisoner found their way to the stake, and soon they were all dead, lining the foot of the mountain and surrounding the chapel. Pleased with this grim state of events, Dracula approached a set table, filled with food. He sat down, pulled up a plate, and enjoyed every bite with the grizzly sight sitting before him.

But not even this satisfied the voivode. On St. Bartholomew's Day, he gave an order to burn two churches, including St. Bartholomew in the village of Codlea. His captain was sent to perform this task, but the locals rebelled and resisted the burning. The captain, with his tail tucked between his legs, returned to Vlad and told him that he had failed. The voivode, not one to tolerate failure well, had the captain impaled on the spot.

"The Forest of Corpses," a Saxon woodcut depicting Dracula having a meal while observing the torture and impalement of his enemies, from the title page of the incunabulum published by Markus Ayrer, Nuremberg, 1499

Discussing the Stakes

Benedict of Boythor was a Polish ambassador in the service of Matthias Corvinus, the king of Hungary. He was dispatched to Wallachia to discuss the matter of settling past aggressions with the Saxons of Transylvania with the current voivode. The king needed his important subjects to get along, which was not an easy task, considering that the Saxons and the Wallachians had been in disputes for years, if not decades. The ambassador reached Dracula's fort, and the two sat to eat dinner. At one point, Vlad ordered that the ambassador stay seated while the voivode's servant ran off to bring something. The corpses strewn across the room had already greatly unnerved the Polish man, but he remained calm enough. Moments later, the servant placed a huge, gelded stake on the table, right next to a serious, unflinching Dracula.

"Tell me, ambassador," the son of Dracul finally spoke, "why do you think I placed this stake on the table right now?"

Deathly afraid but still maintaining his composure, the ambassador replied, "It seems to me, your grace, that a man of some nobility had committed a great crime in your eyes. As such, you want to punish him with a death more honorable than any commoner might deserve."

Still as stern as a rock, the Wallachian autocrat continued, "Indeed, you are correct. You are a royal ambassador to a great and powerful king. Thus, I have made this stake for you."

Wiser than most, Benedict replied, "My lord, if you deem me as someone who has committed a great crime against you, do what you feel is just. You are an impartial judge, and should I die, you will not be the one to blame. The blame is on me and me alone."

A moment or two of silence passed. Soon enough, Vlad burst out laughing, slowly removing the stake. Almost immediately, he ordered that the Polish servant of King Matthias be showered with gifts, riches, and other fineries. "Had you not used those words, my good lord," Dracula said, "you'd have ended up dead upon this stake. You are indeed fit to be an ambassador of great rulers, for you have honed the art of speaking to great rulers. However, other ambassadors should not even dare to do this, not until they've learned the art of speaking to royalty like you."

A Captive of Ill Repute

Upon his fall from power, Vlad, the son of Dracul, had been a prisoner of the Hungarian Crown. But even though he was a prisoner, he was treated like more of an honored guest, someone who could freely walk about the estate, who could converse with barons and lords, and who could taste the finer things in life. But with men of ill repute, rumors tend to rise. Some people claimed that the former voivode had violated a girl and had left her with child. Vlad himself did not like this rumor, so he set about proving his accusers wrong in the most direct way possible. Using a dagger, he cut the poor girl open before the eyes of spectators, moments later showing her open womb and declaring that there was, clearly, no child inside.

Building a Castle

Shortly after reclaiming power in 1456, Vlad wanted to exact revenge on the boyars who had allegedly participated in the expulsion and murder of his father and his older brother. He invited these lords and ladies, as well as their extended family, to dinner one night, possibly on Easter Sunday. After the guests had their fill, Vlad ordered their swift capture. But he didn't immediately have them executed. Instead, he had them march many miles until they reached the almost ruined Poenari Castle. Vlad saw the strategic importance of this fort, so he had every prisoner toil day and night until they fully repaired it. Everyone, from the oldest man to the youngest babe, from the healthiest man to the frailest woman, had to work on rebuilding Poenari, and many of them died trying.

The Turbans

At one point, a delegation from the sultan came to visit Vlad. For years, Vlad had been preventing the Turks from capturing his land and turning it into an Ottoman province. He paid them tribute but refused them other commodities, such as young men and boys for their army. The delegation that arrived wanted to pay their respects to the Wallachian voivode, but Vlad was curious as to why they didn't take off their turbans. The Muslim soldiers replied that it was their custom that the turban always stayed on one's head. In fact, they did not even remove them for the sultan himself. Vlad saw fit to make the Turks keep their word, so he had his soldiers nail the turbans to the Turks' heads.

Vlad and the Priests

Though a religious man, Vlad had no tolerance for priests who did not see eye to eye with him. Two tales speak of his dealings with the men of the cloth.

Once, two priests came from a distant land. The son of Dracul invited them over, willing to have a talk with them. He asked a simple question to the first priest: "What do the people say about me?"

Scared for his life, the first priest mumbled that the people had nothing but words of grace for the voivode. "They think that he is noble and just," the priest said, adding that he was also saying the same things about the monarch. Vlad let him go, but he did not let the priest stray too far. He then asked the same question to the other priest.

"We all have to die someday," the other priest started, "so I'll tell the truth. The people despise you. To them, you are the worst tyrant to have walked the earth, and you've committed countless atrocities that I can't even recount. I know this to be true, for I have spoken with the people about you, and they told me no lies."

Dracula freed this priest, for he was telling the truth. When the other priest was asked the same question again, he simply repeated what the released priest had just said. Vlad had the monk impaled for having lied to him in the beginning.

Another time, a few priests from Gornji Grad (a Catholic convent in modern-day Slovenia) sought refuge in Târgoviște. They were well apprised of Vlad's dealings, but only one priest, Brother Hans, had the courage to confront the voivode. "You tyrant, you murderer, you absolute despot!" the priest cried. "How vile are you to kill innocents? What did the pregnant women do to deserve to be maimed and impaled like that? Or what about the children? Some were only three years old. Others were not even three hours old! Yet you impale them

71

all, healthy and ill alike, young and old alike, both guilty and innocent. Tell me, why kill those who committed no crimes? Why women and children?"

Dracula, of course, had a ready response. "If you need to clean your soil for plowing, you should do it properly and thoroughly. You shouldn't only get rid of the stems of weeds and thorns but also the roots. For, you see, if the roots are left behind, then another dangerous weed will grow, stronger than before. For that reason, I have to weed out my adversaries before they even grow up. These children are those adversaries."

In order to "honor" Brother Hans for his insult, Vlad impaled him personally. Moreover, he didn't use the tried and true method of inserting the stake through the anal cavity. Instead, he forced the sharp stake directly into Brother Hans's forehead. His head was now at the bottom, with his feet in the air, and he thus hung on that stake upside-down, terrifying the other monks so much that a few of them fled, barely surviving to tell the tale.

Sacking Bulgarian Lands

Vlad moved with his army to Nicopolis in 1462. The voivode made short work of the local Jews, Christians, and pagans, slaughtering over 5,000 people, not counting those who burned in the fires. Some of his soldiers spared dozens of maidens and beautiful women, asking the voivode if they could marry them. But Vlad would have none of it. He ordered that all of the soldiers and their women be chopped into pieces with swords and spears, much akin to slicing cabbage.

As a tributary state to the Ottomans, Vlad had to pay a yearly sum of money. He claimed to the Turkish emissaries that he would bring the tribute personally. The Turks, overwhelmed, welcomed him into Bulgaria, arriving on horseback in small groups. Once most of them were there, Vlad enacted his plan and had them all slaughtered. This was an easy task since none of the Ottomans came bearing arms.

Shortly after, the Wallachian voivode would burn Bulgaria to the ground, taking 25,000 lives that day, at the very least.

Portraits and Artistic Depictions of Vlad III

Vlad the Impaler had been somewhat of a celebrity in late medieval Europe. Even during his own life, minstrels and bards would travel the countryside and sing of his exploits at various royal courts. As such, certain rulers became interested in what this monstrous man looked like, so much so that they would pay good money to have his portrait hung on the wall of their castle.

Quite a few portraits of Dracula exist from medieval times, but before we can assess whether or not they match his historical appearance, we need to find out if there was an eyewitness description of the voivode from when he was alive. As luck would have it, there was one person with both the capabilities and proximity to the Impaler who provided a physical description of him.

During Vlad's reign, Hungary, as well as other Catholic Balkan countries, was in frequent correspondence with the pope, usually on the matters of foreign affairs and dealings with heathens. Since the pope operated from Rome, he would send formal legates to various European courts, and these legates would serve as the Catholic representatives of the Holy See. One such legate was a Croatian bishop called Nicholas of Modruš. Nicholas was a learned man who was well-versed in the Glagolitic script and the matters of faith, and he was a papal legate at several European courts, most notably that of the Bosnian king Stephen Tomašević and of the Hungarian king Matthias Corvinus. Considering that Nicholas lived until 1480 and that he had been a court staple throughout his service to Corvinus, he had to have met Dracula at some point in his life.

Upon meeting the voivode for the first time, Nicholas was as fascinated as most people would be. "He was not very tall," begins the legate, "but had indeed been quite stocky and strong, bearing a terrible, cold appearance. He had a strong, aquiline nose, wide nostrils, a reddish, thin face upon which the exceptionally long eyelashes framed his large, wide-open green eyes; those eyes were made threatening with his thick, bushy black eyebrows. Both his face and chin were clean-shaven, except for his notable moustache. The swollen temples appeared to be increasing the bulk of his head. A neck thick as a bull's connected with his head, and from his head hung thick, black, curly locks of hair, falling on his wide-shouldered back."

From this image, we can see that Dracula must have been quite imposing, despite the fact that some of his traits were not those characteristic of a stern, harsh ruler. Usually, medieval nobles like the Serbian emperor Stefan Dušan the Great and the Hungarian general John Hunyadi were described as tall, gallant men. Dracula being described as "not very tall" and "stocky" invokes an image of an everyman rather than a ruler, and his facial characteristics (bushy unkempt brows, thick dark hair, mustache, sunken features) only support that image. However, Nicholas saw it fit not only to describe Vlad in detail but also to provide the pope with some of the earliest stories recorded about him and his cruelty in Wallachia (Nicholas did so as early as 1462, the same year Vlad was imprisoned by King Matthias).

Even though Nicholas didn't capture every single detail about the voivode (like his garb, his posture, etc.), we still have a basic description to go off of when we delve into the many portraits of Vlad. Indeed, almost a dozen portraits of the Impaler have survived from the Middle Ages, which is more than any other Wallachian ruler. But before we discuss those, we need to cover the extraordinary circumstances that led to their creation.

As the stories of the voivode spread throughout Europe, they caught the ear of Ferdinand II, Archduke of Further Austria. Though he had come to power in 1564, which was almost a century after Vlad's death, the archduke had a keen eye for the arts, as was the case with a great number of European nobles during the Renaissance era. An avid collector, Ferdinand moved into Ambras Castle at Innsbruck, using it as his place of residence in 1567. Within the castle walls, he began collecting a wide variety of items such as armor and weaponry, musical instruments, scientific apparatuses, and precious items, as well as various paintings from different artists, well-known and anonymous alike. The castle still stands today, though a great portion of the collection had to be moved to the Kunsthistorisches Museum in Vienna.

Ferdinand II wanted his collection to be as varied and intriguing as possible, which is why we find, among other things, portraits with unusual and morbid undertones, somewhat akin to showcasing circus freaks on canvas. Four portraits, in particular, stand out from the collection. The first is that of Petrus Gonsalvus, or rather Pedro González, a Spanish man with a rare condition known as hypertrichosis. González had an excess of hair growing on his face and all over his body, making him look like a werewolf. He had been a staple of several European courts, most notably that of Parma, Italy, where he had married and become a member of the nobility. Because the portrait's first appearance was at Ambras Castle, the condition we know as hypertrichosis also bears the name "Ambras syndrome"; as an aside, this condition still occurs today, affecting no more than fifty people worldwide.

The next notable portrait is associated with Gregor Baci (though not explicitly so), a Hungarian nobleman who had survived a fatal injury to the head. The portrait itself depicts a man with a lance rammed through his head, more specifically through his right eye socket, with the left eye bulging out unnaturally and bleeding and a small scar on the left side of his shaven scalp. Legend has it that Baci survived a joust and had lived with the spear in his socket for about one year before ultimately succumbing to his injury.

The third in the list of portraits is that of a man with an evident disability. As far as portraits go, this one has an incredibly bizarre composition, showing a man prostrate on the floor, almost naked save for a neckpiece and a hat, both of which look expensive and made for the higher classes. He is looking directly at the viewer, which makes the painting all the more unsettling. When an onlooker analyzes the man's body, they can ascertain that his arms and legs are withered and bent unnaturally to the point of being useless. Initially, the painting contained a red piece of paper covering the body, forcing the viewer to remove the paper and get shocked by the revelation underneath. According to some art critics and historians, the painting probably depicts a court jester since it was not uncommon for people with physical disabilities to entertain monarchs.

However, it is the fourth portrait that we ought to focus on, for it is the most famous artistic depiction of none other than Vlad the Impaler himself. Looking into the middle distance and dressed in a mix of Wallachian and Ottoman garb, the voivode looks every bit as menacing as Nicholas of Modruš described him. There are some discrepancies, such as Vlad being depicted with somewhat fair hair (it's not as dark as Nicholas described it) and with well-groomed eyebrows, but everything else is right there, from the hawkish nose to the wide-open eyes and thick mustache. Notably, the Ambras portrait also shows Dracula with an oversized lower lip, which seems to have been a staple of his portraits at the time.

We should note that the Ambras portrait was painted in the 16th century, well after the Impaler had passed away. However, art historians believe that the portrait is based off on an older painting with only a few stylistic changes. The portrait at Ambras was meant to show the voivode as a "psychogram of evil" rather than just a ruler. And considering the impression it left next to the other three portraits described above, this portrait, made decades after the Impaler's death, is a testament to just how infamous and fascinating he was to the medieval man.

Medieval and Renaissance paintings saw the voivode as a spectacular leitmotif in artwork that featured some sort of grim scene, usually from the Bible. The first known depictions assumed to be those of the Impaler, as seen in the Ambras portrait, were found as early as 1460 when Vlad was still in power at Târgovişte. One such painting is the Calvary of Christ, a fresco in the Maria am Gestade church in Vienna. A man bearing a striking resemblance to Dracula, right down to his robes and headgear, is seen conversing with another person. Another painting, called *Pilate Judging Jesus Christ*, depicts Pilate as the Wallachian voivode, again right down to the robes and headgear. This painting was made in 1463, a year into Vlad's imprisonment at Visegrád. But perhaps the most famous example can be found in the Österreichische Galerie Belvedere museum in Vienna in a painting called *The Martyrdom of Saint Andrew.* Curiously, Dracula is depicted as one of the onlookers, observing Saint Andrew as he is being tortured by three other men. Not only does the appearance of this enigmatic onlooker match that of Dracula, but his apparent enjoyment of the brutal scene was well in line with how the Saxons of Transylvania depicted him to the Viennese people.

And speaking of the Saxons, we have to include the earliest known portraits that actually depicted Dracula in person and didn't use him as a motif in an artistic rendering of a biblical event. These portraits all come from the incunabula printed in the late 15th century, with the earliest surviving copies dating back to 1488 and 1491. On both of these pamphlets, we see the portrait of Dracula, once again looking into the middle distance, with an ornate headdress and elaborate garb. But more importantly, we can see the facial features of the man that terrified so many Saxons back in his day, and once again, we see that everything Nicholas of Modruš said about the voivode (save for a few notable details) fits the description perfectly. This Vlad is just as long-haired, mustachioed, and bug-eyed as the portrait at Ambras depicts him, but we also see the sunken face, the pronounced lower lip, and the thick bushy eyebrows. Even in this stylized form, Dracula shows an imposing, dreadful presence to the viewer, so much so that an average Saxon would gladly read any shred of info on the man.

One of the last known depictions of Vlad during the Renaissance era is from the 17th century, and to date, it is the only Renaissance painting that shows the voivode's full body. Currently on display in the Gallery of Ancestors of the Hungarian House of Esterházy, located in Forchtenstein Castle in Austria, this full-sized portrait shows Vlad as a gaunt, somewhat emaciated man wearing royal garb, with a saber at his hip and a mace in his hand. Though not as detailed as some of the other depictions of the voivode, it certainly follows the trend of showing him as a man of action and morbid mystery, keeping the same bulging eyes and the same aquiline nose.

Of course, not all contemporary depictions of Dracula were consistent. For instance, within the Saxon incunabula, there were depictions of scenes with the Impaler dining in a forest of impaled corpses. While we do see some elements that match the other portraits, such as the mustache, the bulging eyes, and even the headgear to an extent, we also see that the voivode is sporting an unkempt beard. Naturally, having a beard was not uncommon among medieval rulers, Christian and Muslim alike, but Nicholas himself clearly stated the voivode had a clean-shaven appearance and a groomed mustache. We can speculate that the Saxons who departed Transylvania did so at a period where Vlad might have had a beard, but the more likely scenario is that the artist simply did this rendition of the Impaler with a bushy, messy beard to give him more of an insane look. There are even a few woodcuts that show Vlad with short hair and a turban, which is more reminiscent of a Turkish bey or a janissary than a Wallachian lord; even more noteworthy is the absence of that morbid insanity and cruel, calculated stare that came to dominate most Dracula artwork. Instead, here we see a rather content man gazing blissfully forward.

Artistic depictions of Vlad III, both oral and on canvas, were not kind to him. They would almost exclusively come from Germanic sources, so there would always be an air of monstrosity to them that practically dehumanized the voivode. However, the artists who depicted him visually knew to give him that aristocratic gravitas, from the earliest portraits all the way until the Renaissance. Despite his unimpressive description given to us by Bishop Nicholas, we can definitely see an important trait that only someone like Vlad would emanate—that of a man who, despite his appearances, made a dent in human history to the point where he terrified people even centuries after being dead.

Saxon woodcut depicting the portrait of Vlad the Impaler, Nuremberg, 1488

Chapter 5 – The Character of Dracula: Personality Traits, Motivations

Dracula has always been one of those historical figures that fascinate mankind on multiple levels. It's not that much of a stretch to compare him to other popular figures like Hitler, Stalin, Rasputin, Napoleon, Caligula, Gandhi, Alexander the Great, William the Conqueror, Joan of Arc, Einstein, or Ivan the Terrible. As we saw earlier, the public image of the Impaler had been a conversation starter many decades after his death, to the point where some of the biggest European elites were fascinated by him and, arguably, even dreaded him. Moreover, the rekindled interest for the voivode after Bram Stoker published his novel only helped to show that the people of the late 19th century had the same type of passion and fascination that those of the 15th century did, as do the people living today. And that passion has everything to do with how a controversial person acted and, more importantly, why they acted that way.

It's incredibly difficult to discern personality traits of someone who has long been gone. Most of the time, when historians try to give a character profile of a historical figure, they have to piece it together from any number of relevant sources, which is not always easy to do. For example, we can't really say what type of person Aristotle was like since none of his original writings survived, nor are there any written works that describe him in detail. Moreover, we don't have any of his correspondence (like letters and such), so we can't ascertain what kind of views he had and how he acted upon them. On the other hand, we have people like H. P. Lovecraft who wrote tens of thousands of letters, detailing their life and opinions prominently. That's why we know more about Lovecraft, who lived in the early 20th century, than we do about Aristotle, and we still don't know everything about the horror author.

How do these examples relate to Vlad III, however? Well, before we can discern what type of person he was, we need to go over everything we know about his character from the limited information gathered about him. Very few documents issued by or written by Dracula survive, and those that do offer scant clues into his character. Quite literally, more than 90 percent of the sources that mention Dracula are outside of Wallachia, and they often contradict themselves. More importantly, they weren't always written by people who had his best interests in mind. The courtiers at Buda or Catholic monks would frequently refer to the voivode as someone beneath them, while the Saxons would portray him as an outright monster. On the other hand, the Kievan Russians and some of the local Balkan populace would hail him as a hero and a man of virtue. And then there were ancient historians who would merely mention the Impaler in passing, not really providing an opinion one way or the other.

So, in order to make heads or tails of what Dracula was like, we need to provide a few caveats, and they are as follows:

- There is not enough information about this ruler; before any deeper analysis can be conducted, we need to find more contemporary sources that look into Vlad III on a personal level

- Not all of the sources we have on him are reliable; depending on who wrote them, they can differ wildly from the actual person that lived in and ruled over Wallachia in the 15th century

- Aside from the sources, we also need to take into account where Dracula was born, where he lived, the events that shaped his life, the acts he performed during his life, the company he kept, and the legacy he left behind; in other words, we have to let his actions speak for him.

Obviously, the first thing we need to address is the Impaler's supposed extreme cruelty. It's undeniable that the voivode committed numerous acts during his three reigns that people in the 21st century would deem inhumane. Aside from impaling, there were also decapitations, public executions, mutilations, potential genocides, unfair taxation, and open xenophobia, among others. Considering how often these acts occurred during his time on the throne, and how frequently both people sympathetic to his cause and his fiercest detractors spoke of them, a reader would not be judged too harshly if they thought that Vlad III was one of the cruelest people in Europe at the time. But therein lies the misconception. Vlad's cruelty, as heinous as it might have been, was the norm for the time. Both his frequent allies (the Moldavians, Hungarians, Bulgarians) and his enemies (the Ottoman Empire, Wallachian claimants to the throne, Transylvanian upstarts) employed similar, if not the same, methods of punishment. In that sense, we can say that Vlad's cruelty was calculated and very much warranted for the time.

This brings us to a specific personality trait that we can definitely ascribe to the infamous voivode. Namely, Vlad III was possibly one of the shrewdest politicians in the Balkans at the time, more or less on the same level as Skanderbeg, John Hunyadi, Đurađ Branković, Mehmed the Conqueror, and Matthias Corvinus. During his short time in office, Vlad knew exactly what types of measures he needed to employ to keep his realm safe and in one piece. Oftentimes, he would solve disputes and issues with brute force, such as punishing the traitorous boyars who claimed loyalty to any voivode before him if they found it beneficial. Other times, he would settle for lesser forms of punishment, such as banishing his adversaries or issuing edicts that banned trade. But Vlad also exhibited examples of positive behavior. During his reign, the native Wallachians of Transylvania, as well as Wallachia proper, enjoyed a period of relative stability. Laws were enforced, and the average villager felt secure that they wouldn't be mugged or killed out in the open. Dracula also donated vast amounts of wealth to monasteries and, despite his later conversion to Roman Catholicism, was a patron of the Wallachian Orthodox Church. For instance, he gave tax exemptions to the monasteries of Cozia and Tismana, probably expanded the Monastery of Snagov, founded the Comana Monastery as well as a church in the city of Târgşor, and donated graciously to the monasteries at Mount Athos, located in modern-day Greece. In addition, he was most likely instrumental in enabling the Wallachian Orthodox Church to elect its own metropolitan; in his time, metropolitans were elected from the clergy at Constantinople, so his promotion of the abbot of Cozia to the position of a metropolitan singlehandedly gave the Wallachian Church its independence from the Ecumenical Church in the Eastern Roman capital.

We should note that the positive aspects of Vlad's reign, just like the negatives, were not a reflection of him as either a "morally good" or a "morally evil" person. In fact, all of them show just how prudent he was as a ruler. Donating to the churches and monasteries in medieval times was almost a requirement for a ruler. It didn't make matters any easier if you were a child from a religiously mixed marriage (and those were a dime a dozen in an area laden with both Orthodox and Catholic Christian rulers, as well as rulers who belonged to other minor sects of Christianity and Islam). Moreover, if you were a bastard child born out of wedlock or out of infidelity, the Church had the power to sway public opinion against you. And let's not forget that Vlad's father was an illegitimate son of a previous ruler and was, in the eyes of many Wallachians even during the Impaler's reign, an illegitimate successor of the great Basarab name. And to top it all off, Vlad had been in the sultan's court as a child, so fears of him becoming a Turkish vassal and subjugating the Christian majority to Islamic rule were very much warranted. Vlad becoming a patron of the Orthodox Christians was not merely a shrewd decision on his part; realistically speaking, he more or less had no other choice.

However, his intellect was just as notable in foreign affairs. The voivode became an ally of several key players early in his political career. He knew that he had to secure an alliance with the Hungarians and the Moldavians and that he had to pacify the Transylvanian Saxon and Szekler communities. With Moldavia, he didn't have too many issues, considering how long the two realms had collaborated with one another. Vlad knew how to capitalize on these relations; had it not been for his one border disagreement with Stephen the Great, he would have remained in power a lot longer than he did. The Hungarians, on the other hand, were not exactly friends to the Wallachian throne, and Vlad knew that very well. His alliance with the court at Buda was purely out of political interest, considering he needed strong allies against the Turks. At the time, few Balkan-based realms could stand up to the sultan, so Hungary appeared as the logical solution.

And it's his very relationship with the Turks that brings up a key aspect of Vlad III that we can safely say was an important part of his personality—vengefulness. Again, this trait was common with medieval rulers, but knowing what we do about the voivode, we can definitely say that his whole raison d'être was to take vengeance upon the Ottomans. Being taken in as a young boy on the cusp of adolescence by the sultan's forces must have triggered a massive sense of xenophobia in Vlad, a kind obviously not found with his brother Radu. But then again, the two were treated somewhat differently, insofar as Radu was clearly the meek, submissive favorite, and the older Vlad was the upstart who didn't know his place. Gradually, Dracula's outbursts at Edirne would subside, but his hatred for the Ottomans only grew from there. So, when he finally reached power in a more tangible sense, i.e., when he became voivode for a second time, he took a more aggressive stance toward his former captors. Not only did he defy the Ottoman court often, but he would also exact severe punishments upon his captives. Even in his losing battles, Vlad would prove to be a ruthless warrior whom even some of the sternest of Turkish warriors feared.

Of course, his vengeful nature also showed in his dealings with traitors and non-Wallachians. He treated the Transylvanian Saxons in a similar manner as the sultan would with his disloyal subjects, by subjecting them to everything from torture to impalement. And while the stories published by the Saxons decades later definitely have a lot of exaggeration to them, there was a grain of truth to Dracula's supposed cruel treatment of their people while he was in charge. Let's not forget that, even if there is a possibility that he wasn't born there, Vlad certainly did grow up in Transylvania during a period where the Saxons, as subjects, didn't have a lot of love for any Wallachian overlord, and that the ethnic relations were, to put it lightly, tense. In other words, the reason behind Vlad's cruel treatment of the Saxons is the possibility that the Saxons treated him just as badly when he was a youth.

Judging by the contemporary views of the Wallachians, Vlad was harsh but never to the point where he wasn't respected or even admired. Indeed, most contemporary Wallachian, Moldavian, and Slavic sources claim that Vlad was counted among the greatest rulers that his land had ever seen. Not only did he donate graciously to a multitude of monasteries, but his punishments also didn't seem as frequent or as severe when they were directed at his own native folk. Of course, the punishments were still far from being mild or even warranted, but when comparing the treatment of the Wallachians in Vlad's land to that of the Saxons, we can definitely say that his own people were somewhat better off. With that in mind, we can ascertain that Vlad III was, in a medieval sense of the word, a great patriot and loyal to his people. Thanks to his reputation, even the people outside of Wallachia, including members of royalty, feared him and saw him as a force to be reckoned with. Local boyars and noblemen could no longer exploit the system, and interestingly, the lowest classes saw some improvement when it came to their daily lives. Local legends suggest that thanks to Vlad's brutal penalties, thievery had gone down so much that you could leave a chest full of gold outside, and nobody would dare to take it. And while this is most certainly hyperbole, considering it's a rumor from his time, it's not too much of a stretch to claim that his methods worked in favor of the people.

One other key piece of circumstantial evidence to the theory of Vlad being patriotic is the reactions of the common folk. As the years went by, rebellions (the ones not instigated by foreign powers or local pretenders to the throne) were greatly reduced, and Dracula enjoyed a fair amount of loyalty coming from his native Wallachian common folk. It had been a while since they could rally behind a leader who was as consistent and rational as Vlad, despite his bloody habits. In fact, even people today who live in the rural area where Vlad spent most of his life revere him as a national hero, and most of the legends surrounding him there have a positive spin to them. So, without a doubt, we can say that Vlad's dealings with outsiders such as the Saxons and the Turks were partly inspired by his love of the common folk and the desire to do right by them.

Remains of Vlad III's Princely Court, Târgoviște"

Chapter 6 – Dracula's Successors: Descendants of the Impaler

The story of the Impaler is fascinating enough on its own, but historians (as well as lay readers and researchers) often focus on the more prominent aspects of his life, i.e., his imprisonment by the Turks, his bloody reign, his military exploits, his death, and, most notably, his methods of executing law and justice. However, few tend to focus on Vlad's immediate family, as well as his offspring and successors.

As a ruler and a member of the royal family, Vlad had a family history every bit as complicated as that of the most noteworthy monarchs in Europe. He was married at least twice and, as was customary (though not legal or moral by any standard), probably had more than a few mistresses. And while he did die with the reputation of a monster and a tyrant, he did not die without issue. The Drăculeşti line would continue through three major branches, and all three of those were started by the surviving sons of Vlad II Dracul. So, before we move onto discussing Vlad's own progeny, we should quickly cover those of his brothers.

By far the most prominent descendant of Dracul, other than Vlad himself, was his younger brother Radu. A favorite of Mehmed II's court, Radu quickly rose in the Ottoman ranks and became a skilled military commander with a learned background. Some sources even speculate that he had a prominent part in the Siege of Constantinople in 1453, though these are unconfirmed.

Unlike Vlad, Radu was a prominent supporter of the sultan, and when Mehmed's army began invading Wallachia in the early 1600s, he was one of the generals at the forefront. When Vlad was captured and taken to Hungary, the sultan installed Radu as the bey of Wallachia, legitimizing him as the successor of the Impaler. Interestingly, Wallachia had not become a pashaluk (a province governed by a pasha, i.e., a high-ranking Ottoman noble, as an integral part of the empire) but had retained its independence, merely paying the yearly tributes despite the fact that the ruler was possibly the most staunch Ottoman supporter at the time. One notable consequence of Radu's reign is the fact that the *Sipahi* ("cavalrymen") of the Turkish army increased their activity in southern Wallachia, settling there.

Radu would come to clash with Stephen the Great of Moldavia on multiple occasions, with their first battle being at the Soci River for the city of Chilia in 1471. Bizarrely, Stephen would dethrone Radu a grand total of four times, always replacing him with Basarab Laiotă; even more bizarrely, Radu ruled Wallachia on four separate occasions, meaning he was dethroned and replaced by the same man due to the actions of Stephen the Great. But the bizarreness doesn't end there. Radu's only daughter, Maria Voichița, ended up marrying Stephen the Great in 1478, barely a few years after Radu's death. Through her line, Radu's descendants would come to rule over Moldavia, on and off, until the country's subjugation by the Russians. The last recorded descendant of this line died in 1704.

The other brother that had ruled over Wallachia in the Impaler's time was Vlad IV, known as Vlad the Monk. Some sources state that he was either a legitimate or an illegitimate son of Vlad II Dracul, but there is no definitive proof to either claim. Unlike his brothers, Vlad IV would not openly vie for the throne until the 1480s, when both

Vlad III and Radu had long been dead. He would end up ruling longer than both of them, a little over thirteen years in total.

His own sobriquet, "the Monk," doesn't have a definite source. He was either an incredibly pious ruler, which was not uncommon at the time, or he simply dressed in priestly garb to avoid being killed for political purposes during Vlad's and Radu's turbulent reigns. He himself would dethrone (and be dethroned once by) Basarab IV Țepeluș ("the Little Impaler"), a descendant of the House of Dănești, but Vlad IV would ultimately be succeeded by his son, known to history as Radu IV the Great. Vlad IV's descendants would come to rule both Wallachia and Moldavia, as well as Transylvania, at certain points in history. His own line of the House of Drăculești would see thirteen voivodes succeed him:

- Radu IV the Great
- Vlad V the Younger (also known as *Vlăduț*)
- Radu of Afumați
- Radu Bădica
- Vlad VI Înecatul ("The Drowned")
- Vlad Vintilă de la Slatina
- Radu VII Paisie
- Mircea Ciobanul ("The Shepherd")
- Pătrașcu the Good
- Petru the Younger
- Vintilă, son of Pătrașcu
- Petru II Cercel
- Mihai Viteazul ("The Brave")

Naturally, Vlad III's successors didn't stand idly by during the post-Dracula years of Wallachia's history. The Impaler had two wives, with his second wife being Jusztina Szilágyi and the first still unknown to historians. Some speculate that she had been an illegitimate daughter of John Hunyadi, which would make Vlad's descendants with her potential candidates to the Hungarian throne. Other experts claim that Vlad probably never married the noblewoman in question.

Whatever the case may be, these two marriages produced three sons. Vlad's second son's name doesn't appear in any official records, and the boy died at some point before 1486. The youngest son, also called Vlad, had been a minor noble in the court of the Hungarian king Vladislaus II, a member of the Jagiellonian dynasty and the direct successor to Matthias Corvinus. At some point in 1495, while stationed in southern Transylvania, Vlad began raiding the lands and became a contender for the throne held by Radu the Great. King Vladislaus ordered Vlad to cease all activities and move to the Banat region. Vlad acquiesced, and after his departure of Wallachia, he lived and died as a minor noble. However, the younger Vlad did manage to establish a new house within Hungary, known as the House of Sinteşti. Some of his descendants include Ludovicus Drakulya, his own two sons called Ladislaus (or Vlad) and John, and Ladislaus's son John Dracula de Band. John was the last known male descendant of Vlad's Sinteşti line, though the female descendants who bore the Dracula name survived well into the 18th century.

Another interesting case of a potential descendant of Dracula was a certain Russian priest called Vasian. Apparently, he had been a descendant of the families who fled from Wallachia (or Moldavia) to Russia and had styled himself with the signature of "Vasian, surnamed Dracula" while copying a 1512 chronicle in 1538. It's unclear whether he was really a descendant of Dracula, but if we were to assume that he was, he would have likely been a bastard child born out of wedlock.

By far the most prominent descendants of Vlad the Impaler came through his eldest son, Mihnea cel Rău ("The Evil"). As a staunch opponent of the Turks, Mihnea was incredibly similar to his father in terms of cruelty toward the disloyal boyars. Reports unfavorable to Mihnea state that he confiscated boyar property frequently, slept with their wives, worked the men to the bone, cut off the noses and lips of those who opposed him, and either hung or drowned the rest. Most of these stories come from the Craioveşti boyars, who were his open adversaries, so they ought to be taken with a grain of salt. However, even if they are taken at their word, that would still make Mihnea not as infamous or as bloodthirsty as his late father.

Mihnea only ruled between 1508 and 1510, having fled Wallachia when the boyars revolted. His son, Mircea III, briefly ruled the land before being deposed by Vlad the Younger, while his other son, Miloș, had no prominent role in courtly affairs at the time. Mihnea's only daughter, Ruxandra, married the Moldavian prince Bogdan III cel Orb ("The One-Eyed"). After fleeing Wallachia, Mihnea settled in Sibiu, in his father's old home, and soon converted to Catholicism. One morning, he was leaving the Dominican Holy Cross church after a mass and was cornered by a group of 33 hired assassins. He was killed on the spot by Dimitrije Jakšić, a Serbian noble whose daughter Mihnea had raped while in power. Both Jakšić and the other 32 men were of the Craiovești boyar faction.

Mircea III, Dracula's grandson, might not have ruled for long, but he did have several noteworthy descendants. They were Alexander, Peter, and Miloș. Of the three, Miloș would be the only one who did not become a ruler. Since he was born with a withered arm, he spent his days as a professor in the patriarchal school of Constantinople and enjoyed great prestige among the Greek intellectual elites. He was also credited as the founder of the monastery of Nea Mone on Chios in 1573.

Peter, known as Peter the Lame due to a physical deformity, would become the prince of Moldavia without initially even knowing of his Wallachian origins, having been raised by the Turks his whole life. Since Peter was a weak ruler, he would be dethroned twice, but he left it willingly the third time after falling in love with a Romani woman named Irina. The two moved to Bolzano, a city in the present-day Italian province of Tyrol, where Peter fell in love with another woman, a Circassian lady-in-waiting called Maria. She would give him an heir, Ștefăniță, who never ascended the throne. Peter died of syphilis in 1594 and was buried in Bolzano.

Alexander II Mircea was, therefore, the most prominent of Vlad III's great-grandchildren to ascend to the Wallachian throne, which

Alexander did in 1568 (and then again in 1574). Soon after his coronation, he showed the same tendencies his ancestor had, decapitating over 200 boyars the very next month after his coronation. Several other massacres followed throughout his reign, and Alexander would, eventually, die in 1577, possibly due to poisoning by unsatisfied boyars. Aside from his massacres, Alexander was also known for imposing a ridiculous tax on unfertile sheep, as well as founding several stunning monasteries near Bucharest and Craiova.

Alexander's son, Mihnea II, would ascend the throne at twelve years of age, with his mother acting as a regent. They ruled until 1583, and they are remembered as extremely unpopular rulers, as they increased taxes constantly and continued the cruel policies of Alexander II. Mihnea was deposed in favor of Petru II Cercel and was held captive by the Ottomans, but his mother managed to buy favor with the sultan to have Mihnea reclaim the throne. During his next rule, from 1585 to 1591, Mihnea became even more infamous to the local Wallachians, so the Ottomans deposed him, this time in favor of Ştefan Surdul, a supposed harness maker and leather cutter. Humiliated, Mihnea tried vying for the Moldavian throne with no success and even went so far as to convert himself and his eldest son to Islam, taking the name Mehmed Bey. This political move earned him the sobriquet Turcitul ("The Islamized"), as well as the governorship of the sanjak ("district") of Nicopolis in Bulgaria. Despite these measures, he would die without reclaiming the Wallachian throne in 1601, buried in an unmarked grave.

Interestingly, Mihnea II's oldest son did not succeed him to the throne of Wallachia. That honor went to his youngest son, Radu Mihnea, and more importantly, the young voivode achieved this feat in 1601, the same year Mihnea died unceremoniously. Radu was possibly the most beloved ruler to descend from Dracula, having been an educated man of culture, a lover of the arts, and a great unifier who would come to rule both Wallachia and Moldavia, as well as Transylvania, a feat that was achieved only by one ruler before him, Voivode Mihai the Brave.

Radu Mihnea was instrumental during the peace of Hotin in 1621, which was concluded between the Ottomans (of whom Radu was the vassal) and the Poles. Both sides praised the ruler's prowess and ingenuity and were grateful for his mediation of the treaty. Aside from his diplomatic skills, Radu was also a great friend of the Orthodox Church, having gifted numerous monasteries, including the ones he was educated in. He died from gout in 1626 when he was 42 years old.

The last two descendants of Dracula who held any power in Wallachia were Alexandru Coconul ("The Child") and Mihnea III. Little is known of either, other than the fact that Alexandru ruled between 1623 and 1627 as a voivode of Wallachia and between 1629 and 1630 as a prince of Moldavia, while Mihnea III ruled Wallachia between 1658 and 1659, thus making him the last official ruler of the land who came directly from Dracula's male line.

Of course, the story of Dracula's descendants doesn't necessarily end there. At some point in Romania in the 1950s, a news article stated that the final descendant of the male line of Dracula had passed away a day earlier. However, people claiming to be the direct descendants of Vlad the Impaler were not a new phenomenon in Romania. In fact, some Romanian historians even claim to be descended from Vlad's bloodline. However, it might be possible that his successors through the female line still live to this very day.

Radu Mihnea, descendant of Vlad III, image over his tombstone, from Radu Voda Monastery, Bucharest[ii]

Chapter 7 – Legacy of Dracula: Historical Importance, Bram Stoker's Novel, Popular View Today

The Historical Importance of Vlad the Impaler

Students of history will know how to recognize the importance of an event or a sequence of events not just out of emotional reasons (i.e., because they happen to like a certain individual) but out of an overall sense of historical cause and effect. As an example, let's take the fall of the Western Roman Empire in 476. To us, it marked the end of an era, a shift from the classical period to medieval times, with drastically different outlooks on life, customs, daily affairs, etc. Now, these differences are not so drastic when you actually live through them; to the average Roman citizen, the fall of Rome was a tragic event, but they didn't suddenly stop being Roman just because they lost their independence to a barbarian king. Indeed, to them, as brutal as it was, the fall of the empire was simply another day. The same goes for all events we deem historic and groundbreaking. However, that doesn't diminish their historical importance in the grand scheme of things, no matter how small their contribution seems to be.

When you study the medieval Balkans, you understand just how important this region is for the entire history of Europe, all thanks to individuals and events that occurred on this small peninsula. The Fall of Constantinople, for example, was an event that still echoes worldwide, as it represented the end of an era and resulted in a huge Muslim expansion in the East. That same expansion was greatly reduced by some important events happening before (the Battle of Kosovo in 1389) and after the fall (Skanderbeg's wars against the Turks, John Hunyadi's campaigns). Had it not been for these minor Balkan countries, the Ottoman expansion would definitely have come more rapidly, and the geopolitical map of Europe as we know it today would look drastically different.

In that sense, Vlad III was possibly one of the most important figures of his age. His shrewdness and cruelty aside, he was one of the few rulers at the time who could stand up to the Ottomans in an effective, meaningful way and manage to protect the smallfolk in the process. Though he didn't reign for more than six years, a figure which includes all three of his reigns, he definitely made an impact on the people at the time. His enemies grew to fear his tenacity and his propensity to do everything in his power to win. It's rare to see a minor noble like Vlad (for, in the grand scheme of things and looking at it objectively, he was a minor noble) stir up so much fear in the sultan of what was becoming the biggest empire in medieval times, the same sultan who had sacked a holy city not long ago (Constantinople's fall was still within living memory when Dracula came to power).

However, it's also rare to see just how much of an impact a supposed tyrant had on the common folk. Yes, they definitely feared him, much more than his successors (some of whom committed acts arguably just as cruel), but there was a trend growing among the Wallachian non-gentry, a trend that saw a rehabilitation of sorts of the Impaler. Villagers soon began to weave tales of their own concerning the voivode, and villages around the areas where he either dwelled or passed away started getting renamed, bearing either his own name or his sobriquet. To this very day, Romanian folklore in these areas is heavy with Dracula's spirit weighing it down, and the rural folks of Romania still fear him as if he had never died.

Folklore, like official historical documents, books, and letters, is incredibly important to modern historians. Dismissing folk tales about Dracula, or any historical figure, as simple fiction is by no means the right thing to do when studying history. Naturally, you need to take into account that there will be heavy distortions and changes, considering most of the folklore is passed down through oral tradition, and nothing from contemporary folklore should be believed at face value. But folklore, in and of itself, can serve as a good starting point in finding historical facts and even figuring out the potential thought processes and attitudes of the people living several hundred years ago. Some of the greatest discoveries (the city of Ur, the labyrinth at Knossos, the city of Troy) were made thanks to the archeologists and researchers taking written and oral legends into account. The same goes for Vlad III; though the legends about him may exaggerate numbers and get more than a few names wrong, some of the basic questions about his life and times can be answered by analyzing these folk myths to find scraps of useful, logical information.

Artistic Influence; Bram Stoker and His Novel

Even when Vlad was alive, the tales of his cruel acts had reached the ears of many prominent artists. Painters such as the German Renaissance artist Matthias Grünewald and the Swiss painter Niklaus Manuel Deutsch prominently depicted death and gory scenes in their work, with Deutsch even portraying a brutal group impaling in his painting *The Martyrdom of the Ten Thousand*. It became quite an evident trend among the Germanic Renaissance authors, these depictions of gruesome deaths and graphic imagery, and it's not that far-fetched to claim that these painters, among others, had read the incunabula containing the stories of Vlad the Impaler since they were very much in print during the artists' lifetimes.

Other artists of later centuries also tried their hands at depicting gruesome scenes, though when it came to Dracula himself, he underwent a slight shift from a tyrant to a pragmatic yet cruel leader fighting for independence. The interest for the Wallachian voivode would have died down had it not been for a novel by an Irish writer that, unwittingly, put the old monarch back into the limelight, though not in the best of ways.

Bram Stoker published his novel, *Dracula*, in 1897. The novel was not an immediate hit, though Victorian readers did receive it positively, embracing it as a good adventure story. However, Stoker almost unwittingly spearheaded a new "school of thought" on Vlad the Impaler, ascribing to him a number of misattributions that sometimes went completely contrary to historical facts. As Stoker himself stated, he knew next to nothing on the voivode, and what limited knowledge he had on Wallachia, he based on a somewhat obsolete source, a book published in 1820 with the title *Account of the Principalities of Wallachia and Moldavia with Political Observations Relative to Them* by William Wilkinson. Stoker's interest was simply to write a good novel featuring vampires after being inspired by an article about Transylvanian vampiric activity that had been published two years prior. In fact, the main villain of the piece wasn't even called "Dracula" in his early drafts and instead bore the name *Count Wampyr*.

There are quite a few misconceptions about Vlad III that were a direct result of Stoker's novel becoming more and more popular over the years, so much so that actual historians took them at face value. Some of the more egregious ones are the following:

- In the novel, Dracula is a count; there is no title of "count" when it comes to either Wallachian or Transylvanian rulers. Vlad was a voivode (the roughest equivalent to that is "prince" or "duke").

- In the novel, Dracula is of Szekler origin; Vlad was actually Wallachian, from a long and established list of Wallachian rulers.

- In the novel, Dracula rules over Transylvania; while Vlad was born in Transylvania and did have both political and personal investment in the region, he was the ruler of Wallachia.

- In the novel, Dracula is portrayed as a bloodthirsty vampire, which his subjects are aware of it; vampirism is a widespread phenomenon throughout the Balkans even today, but no contemporary source actually references vampirism when talking about Vlad III.

Of course, readers (and even contemporary historians) can't be too harsh on Stoker; he was merely writing a novel with fantastical elements, and he decided to borrow the name of an infamous ruler from a distant land that would hopefully entice readers and pique their interest. Notably, Stoker did include a few passing references about Vlad's life in the novel, which were somewhat factually accurate. For instance, his characters discuss Dracula's victory over the Turks at a river that formed a natural border between the two nations. Considering Vlad's extensive warfare on the Danube, this nugget of information on Stoker's part is not false. The same goes for Stoker retelling parts of Dracula's life story, where he had been betrayed by his own brother who was loyal to the Turks. Once again, knowing what we know about Radu the Handsome and the final years of Vlad's second reign, we can commend Stoker for including that bit within the novel.

Ultimately, while Stoker's novel did cause harm to the historical research into Vlad the Impaler (to the point where his sobriquet, "Dracula," wasn't even used by official history books until after the novel had become popular), it also had a positive effect. More and more people became interested in the history of both Romania and Transylvania, which spearheaded the efforts of some scholars of Romanian studies to delve deeper into the House of Drăculeşti. As of today, the field of Romanian history has greatly expanded, and new discoveries about Dracula's time are being made almost every year, and it's in no small part thanks to Stoker sparking interest through his fiction.

Bram Stoker, circa 1906[iii]

Dracula Today: A View of the Impaler in Modern Times

Views of the Wallachian voivode fluctuated quite a bit in the 19th century, ranging from seeing him as a murderer and a sadist (a view no doubt inspired by the original Saxon texts) or as a benevolent leader who had to commit cruel acts (inspired by Wallachian folklore and the Slavic texts).

Interestingly, Communist Romania would elevate Vlad as a national hero but only doing so within the service of the Party and with heavy historical inaccuracies. Books, studies, papers, and treatises were written exalting the voivode and extolling his many virtues, painting him as the perfect Romanian national hero and, astonishingly, even justifying some of his brutal acts. Nicolae Ceaușescu himself, the president of the Socialist Republic of Romania and the country's most notorious dictator, saw Vlad as the perfect role model that a ruler should aspire to be, frequently saying so publicly. However, this view of the Impaler dealt a powerful blow to Romanian historiography at the time; lots of scholarly written material was censored or outright banned because it portrayed Vlad "in a negative light," i.e., it spoke both of his accomplishments and his atrocities. The situation regarding these historical revisions would not end until the regime change in 1989, and even then, it was a gradual climb back to regain some semblance of objectivity and historicity.

The 21st-century view of Vlad the Impaler is, therefore, one of pure scholarly fascination. Some political groups label his acts as hate crimes and genocides, but these are viewed through the lens of modern politics, and such opinions are not to be taken into consideration when discussing historical validity to any claims about the voivode. The interest in Vlad the Impaler has not waned among Romanian historians and researchers, and the relevant field of studies on the subject is constantly growing, especially since the Romanian intellectual elite has gained access to some of the latest research methods, as well as connections with professional historical institutes from across the globe, all in the interest of learning everything there is to know about the son of Dracul and his turbulent life.

Vlad the Impaler and the Turkish Envoys, *painted by Theodor Aman, oil on canvas, from National Museum of Romania, 1886*[iv]

Conclusion

Fans of the fictional Dracula, now a staple of modern horror and a pop culture icon, may find it difficult to reconcile that image with the wide-eyed, stern, and haunting visage of the historical Vlad III the Impaler. In many ways, the Wallachian monarch is far more intriguing than the vampire count, with his life constantly ebbing and flowing, remaining full of thrills and excitement until the very end. But then again, truth, as they say, is stranger than fiction.

And indeed, a brief overview of Vlad's life does seem strange and unlikely, especially for a medieval minor noble. How many rulers can attest to being captured as a child by the Ottomans, raised there, then taking the throne for themselves, losing it once, retaking it again, murdering hundreds of thousands of people and successfully repelling the same captors that held him prisoner years ago (captors whose country was almost ten times the size of his), losing the throne again, being captured by a former ally's son, being released by that same person (and marrying his cousin, no less), winning war after war in reclaiming his country, retaking the throne again, and losing it for the final time in the heat of battle? How many rulers can say that they had so many stories written, spoken, and sung about him, or paintings painted of him that ended up in some of Europe's wealthiest castles, that it ended up terrifying some of Europe's most powerful rulers?

And most importantly, how many rulers can attest that they had, in a sense, become the ruler of the people despite enacting some of the most monstrous punishments in human history?

Dracula was, more or less, a product of his time. With all of the nuances and context, we can see that he merely exaggerated his deeds, something other rulers before (and even after) him had done. The short period of his reign is almost disproportionate to the number of acts he committed, wars he fought, people he killed, people he protected, and locations he either visited or dwelled in. The mere fact that he still survives in Romanian folklore is more than enough to tell you just how much of an impact he has had on human history. He was a man who could impale hundreds of people in a single day just because they irked him a little bit, or cut down a trusted general or a staunch supporter for simply making an honest mistake. But he was also a man who could provide troops to protect his people, pass laws that would make it easier for his fellow Wallachians to trade without unfair competition, and both build and gift numerous monasteries to the same Church that probably didn't take too kindly to him. Ironically enough, Vlad was also a monarch who quite literally used underhanded means and barbaric acts to weed out corruption at the very top, and he did so effectively. And thanks to his prudent nature, he would take his long-overdue vengeance on the Ottomans over and over again, beating and humiliating them to the point of desperation.

Of course, we shouldn't romanticize Vlad the Impaler. In the end, he was a human being who committed horrible deeds for both personal and political reasons, which makes him comparatively less of a monster than, for example, some of the 20th-century's worst dictators. But we shouldn't exclude him from the history books either. Even modern rulers can learn a thing or two from Vlad's example (obviously avoiding all of the slaughter) and, in doing so, manage to run a country in a way that makes the little guy feel safer.

Bibliography and References

Akeroyd, J. (2009): The Historical Dracula: Monster or Machiavellian Prince?, In *History Ireland* Vol. 17, No. 2, (pp. 299-315). Dublin, IE: Wordwell Ltd.

Babinger, F. (1992): *Mehmed the Conqueror and His Time.* Princeton, NJ, USA: Princeton University Press

Cazacu, M. (2011): *Dracula.* Leiden, NL & Boston, MA, USA: Brill

Encyclopedia Britannica (1981), Retrieved on May 21st 2020, from https://www.britannica.com

McNally, R. T. & Florescu, R. (1989): *Dracula, Prince of Many Faces: His Life and His Times.* New York, NY, USA: Hachette Book Group

McNally, R. T. & Florescu, R. (1994): *In Search of Dracula: The History of Dracula and Vampires.* Boston, MA, USA: Mariner Books

Mihajlović, K. (2010): *Memoirs of a Janissary.* Princeton, NJ, USA: Markus Wiener Publishers

Perić, Z. et al. (2013): From Wallachian Duke to the Prince of Darkness, In *Researches Review of the Department of Geography, Tourism and Hotel Management* No. 42, (pp. 139-151). Novi Sad, RS: University of Novi Sad, Faculty of Sciences, Department of Geography, Tourism and Hotel Management

Nandriş, G. (1959): A Philological Analysis of "Dracula" and Rumanian Place-Names and Masculine Personal Names in –a/-ea, In *The Slavonic and East European Review,* Vol. 37, No. 89, (pp. 371-377). London, UK: University of London, School of Slavonic and East European Studies

Nandriş, G. (1966): The Historical Dracula: The Theme of His Legend in the Western and in the Eastern Literatures of Europe, In *Comparative Literature Studies* Vol. 3, No. 4, (pp. 367-396). University Park, PA, USA: Penn State University Press

Radin, A. (1998): History, Legend, Literature: Prince Vlad Tepes alias Count Dracula, In *BALCANICA - Annual of the Institute for Balkan Studies* Vol. 29, (pp. 237-258). Belgrade, RS: Serbian Academy of Sciences and Arts, Institute for Balkan Studies

Treptow, K. W. (Ed.) (2018): *Dracula: Essays on the Life and Times of Vlad the Impaler.* Las Vegas, NV, USA: Histria Books

Wikipedia (January 15, 2001), Retrieved on May 21st 2020, from www.wikipedia.org/

Here's another book by Captivating History
that you might be interested in

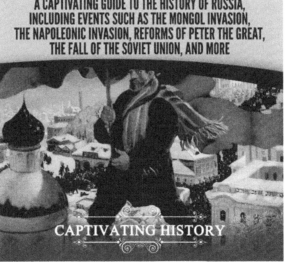

RUSSIAN HISTORY

A CAPTIVATING GUIDE TO THE HISTORY OF RUSSIA,
INCLUDING EVENTS SUCH AS THE MONGOL INVASION,
THE NAPOLEONIC INVASION, REFORMS OF PETER THE GREAT,
THE FALL OF THE SOVIET UNION, AND MORE

CAPTIVATING HISTORY

Notes on Images

[xii] Original image uploaded by Maxpushka on 27 January 2019. Retrieved from https://commons.wikimedia.org/ on May 2020 under the following license: Creative Commons Attribution-ShareAlike 4.0 International. This license lets others remix, tweak, and build upon your work even for commercial reasons, as long as they credit you and license their new creations under the identical terms.

[viii] Original image uploaded by CoolKoon on 17 April 2012. Retrieved from https://commons.wikimedia.org/ on May 2020 under the following license: *Public Domain.* This item is in the public domain, and can be used, copied, and modified.

[ix] Original image uploaded by Dbachmann on 11 September 2011. Retrieved from https://commons.wikimedia.org/ May 2020 under the following license: *Public Domain.* This item is in the public domain, and can be used, copied, and modified.

[x] Original image uploaded by Unibond on 31 December 2016. Retrieved from https://commons.wikimedia.org/ on May 2020 under the following license: *Public Domain.* This item is in the public domain, and can be used, copied, and modified.

[xi] Original image uploaded by CristianChirita on 23 September 2011. Retrieved from https://commons.wikimedia.org/ on May 2020 under the following license: Creative Commons Attribution-ShareAlike 3.0 Romania. This license lets others remix, tweak, and build upon your work even for commercial reasons, as long as they credit you and license their new creations under the identical terms.

[xii] Original image uploaded by Alex:D on 20 June 2007. Retrieved from https://commons.wikimedia.org/ on May 2020 under the following license: *Public Domain.* This item is in the public domain, and can be used, copied, and modified.

[xiii] Original image uploaded by Alexis Jazz on 19 July 2018. Retrieved from https://commons.wikimedia.org/ on May 2020 under the following license: *Public Domain.* This item is in the public domain, and can be used, copied, and modified.

[xiv] Original image uploaded by Bogdan on 31 July 2006. Retrieved from https://commons.wikimedia.org/ on May 2020 under the following license: *Public Domain.* This item is in the public domain, and can be used, copied, and modified.

Made in the USA
Monee, IL
17 December 2021

85960763R00069